Making the News

Making the News

An essential guide for
effective media relations

John Longhurst

NOVALIS

© 2006 Novalis, Saint Paul University, Ottawa, Canada

Cover images: Jupiter Images

Layout: Christiane Lemire

Business Office:

Novalis

10 Lower Spadina Avenue, Suite 400

Toronto, ON M5V 2Z2

Phone: 1-800-387-7164

Fax: 1-800-204-4140

E-mail: cservice@novalis-inc.com

www.novalis.ca

Library and Archives Canada Cataloguing in Publication

Longhurst, John

   Making the news : an essential guide to media relations / John
Longhurst. – Updated ed.

ISBN 2-89507-714-2

   1. Nonprofit organizations–Public relations. 2. Church public relations.
3. Church publicity. I. Title.

HM1221.L65 2006   659.2'88   C2006-900158-8

Printed in Canada.

We acknowledge the financial support of the Government of Canada through the Book
Publishing Industry Development Program (BPIDP) for our publishing activities.

5 4 3 2 1   10 09 08 07 06

Contents

Acknowledgments

I would like to acknowledge and thank the Centre for Faith and the Media, whose generous support made possible the publication of this updated edition of *Making the News*. For more information about the centre, contact

Centre for Faith and the Media
P.O. Box 5694, Station "A"
Calgary, Alberta T2H 1Y1
Tel: 1-877-210-0077
Website: www.faithandmedia.org

John Longhurst
Winnipeg, Manitoba
December 2005

Introduction

Those of us who work for non-profit organizations are faced with a never-ending challenge: how to tell the largest number of people about our events, programs and issues for the least amount of money.

Unlike big corporations, businesses and some special-interest groups, we don't have large budgets that allow us to design and publish advertisements in newspapers and magazines or create commercials for radio and TV. Some of us have no budget for this kind of thing at all!

But having little or no money doesn't mean that we can't share our messages with large numbers of people. We just have to do it differently, by working with the media. We supply media outlets with the thing they need – news – and they give us access to readers, viewers and listeners.

Learning how to work with the media is the purpose of this manual. In it you will find information about how to write a news release, whom to send it to, what time of the day and week to send it. You'll also learn some of the rules editors and reporters live by, and what they look for in a news story.

This revised and updated edition of *Making the News* also features an expanded chapter on religion and the media that deals with some of the unique challenges facing faith groups that want to work with the media.

Working with the media has its risks and challenges, but so does *not* working with the media. If you want to get your message out, attract new supporters or improve the way the media covers your issue, then you will want to work with the media. As an old saying goes, "If you always do what you've always done, you'll always get what you've always gotten."

This manual is for people who want more than what they've always gotten when it comes to communicating their messages through the media.

1

The Media

Why work with the media?

If you are reading this book, you don't need to be convinced of the need to work with the media. But maybe not everyone in your organization is convinced. Maybe the executive director, chair of the board or bishop you report to has had a bad experience with a reporter and doesn't want anything to do with the media ever again. Or maybe he or she sees the media as the enemy, as being opposed to the very things your group stands for, or perhaps is worried about saying the wrong thing in an interview.

Unfortunately, this approach only guarantees further misunderstanding and poor coverage. It also cuts your organization off from the very people you want to share your messages with – the public. By working with the media, you can find new supporters, create understanding for your group or issue and also enable the media to do a better job.

So if someone asks why your organization or faith group should work with the media, here are some good reasons.

1. You have something to say

When it comes to the issue your organization is involved in, you are the expert. You have experience that no one else can match. Your point of view is unique. This qualifies you to speak to the media. After all, news organizations cannot employ people who are experts on every issue, need, health concern or faith group. To do their job, reporters have to talk to people who can offer credible, informed points of view on these and many other important topics – people like you.

2.   Media outlets reach a large number of people

Your magazine or newsletter is an important vehicle of communication, but it only reaches a few people, almost all of whom already are your supporters. If you want to reach out beyond your supporters, you must use the media. Since almost everyone accesses the media in one way or another – through daily newspapers, radio, TV or magazines – there is simply no better way to place your information in front of many people. A single article in a large daily newspaper can reach 100,000 people or more. If the article gets placed on the wire services, it could reach many hundreds of thousands more in other parts of the country. Media coverage gives you a reach that is impossible to achieve through other avenues.

3.   Media outlets reach a broad audience

The most common criticism of many non-profit organizations is that they preach to the converted. That is, important points of view about the world are available only through organizational publications – the kinds of things that are primarily read by people who already share the concerns and support the cause. But people who need to be challenged by your messages – who need to change their minds about your group and what it believes, who need to change their attitudes or actions, or who need to know how they can become involved in your issue – likely do not read your publications. To reach them, you must send your message through the media they use. You must go out and find them; you cannot expect them to somehow find you.

4.   Your supporters notice news coverage about your organization

At first glance, this might not be obvious. After all, is it not just non-supporters who learn about you through the media? Your supporters already read your publications. The truth is that working with the media is an excellent way to reach the people who support you now. Why? The answer is as simple as the old saying about not seeing the forest for the trees. After a while, your supporters become so familiar with your publications and messages that they cease to take notice of them.

But if an article about your group appears in the newspaper, or if a report appears on TV or radio, it's like a flashing beacon attracting their attention, and they will read, watch or listen. To put it another way, I almost never hear supporters comment on articles I write for my organization's publications. But if I am on radio or TV or in the newspaper, they will always tell me that they heard, saw or read about me.

The situation is the same for faith groups. A recent Canadian poll found that 45 per cent of respondents look to the non-religious media for information about their faith groups, not to their denominational periodicals.

5.   Being in the media offers credibility

You know that your group is doing good work. You know that your views are credible. But the people you want to reach don't know that. Sending them your material sometimes isn't enough. Marketing surveys routinely show that people distrust advertising, particularly the ads that claim to offer "unsolicited" endorsements of products. However, people tend to show a higher level of trust for what they read or hear reported as news, because they believe that information reported by the media has been screened for bias by a neutral party. In other words, an article in your publication that praises your efforts or supports your cause will be viewed skeptically by non-supporters – what else would you expect an organization to say about itself? However, if a report in the media praises your organization, or reports about it positively, then the report is seen as being more believable since it is written by a neutral party (someone who has no personal stake in the organization). In other words, it becomes more credible.

6. It's free

It is expensive to purchase advertising in the media. A news report, however, doesn't cost anything. A report about your organization that occupies a quarter of a page in a newspaper or takes a minute of air time can be worth hundreds or thousands of dollars, money you didn't have to pay to get that space or time.

7. Sometimes you can't afford not to work with the media

Murphy's law – "If something can go wrong, it will" – applies to non-profit organizations as well as people. Despite your best efforts, there will be times when things happen that reflect negatively on your organization. You can help mitigate the negative impact of these situations by maintaining regular contact with the media. By establishing a relationship with members of the media, you can help them place the problem in its proper context. A problem can then be seen as an aberration, not as an ongoing difficulty. By maintaining regular contact with the media, you can ensure that the first mention of your organization, or the only mention in a given year, is not a negative one.

8. Reporters and editors need you

In the wake of the US savings and loan scandal in the late 1980s, many people wondered how such a huge financial debacle could have occurred without the media reporting more about it. One US reporter answered by saying that the members of the media couldn't understand the complicated financial material behind the scandal; no one had been available to explain it to them. "We usually depend on governmental institutions or groups like Common Cause or Ralph Nader or somebody to make sense out of all this data for us," he said.

In other words, the media needs groups such as yours as much as you need them. This comes as a surprise to some non-profit groups, since they often view obtaining coverage as the media doing them a favour. Nothing could be further from the truth! The media desperately needs something you have – news and opinion about your involvement in issues that affect your community. It doesn't need it every day, or even every month, of course. But when reporters come to work they have another story to write, or another news show to prepare. Where are they going to find items to fill the space and time? From you. The media needs you to help them make sense of the issue and find people to comment intelligently on it.

This is especially true for religious groups. Many people today are not familiar with religion. They did not grow up going to religious services. They have no innate knowledge about various holy books or doctrines. Some of these people work in the media. If they are to understand your beliefs or practices, you have to tell them. They depend on you to help them through the maze of denominations, splinter groups and doctrinal differences, and a host of other things.

9. Media outlets aren't divine

How is it that news organizations seem to know so many things that are happening in your community? Because someone took the time to tell them. Each day hundreds of news releases pour into newsrooms, letting the media know what is happening or what groups think about various issues. This is their lifeline to the community. If you are not sending your news to the media, reporters and editors will never know what you are doing or even who you are. If reporters don't know who you are, you won't be among their lists of contacts – they won't call for a comment or opinion when a story about your issue or cause comes up. As one reporter said, "I'm not divine. I can't write about things unless someone talks to me."

10. The people you serve or advocate for need you to speak for them

If your group serves poor people in North America or around the world, you are probably aware that one characteristic of poverty is lack of power. One aspect of a lack of power is the inability to interpret your own life – having no control over your story or image, being unable to make yourself heard.

Reporters and editors are not uninterested in the stories of poor people. It's just that people who are poor sometimes don't have the ability to attract the media to tell their story, unless a tragedy happens in their community (e.g., a tragic fire that exposes substandard housing or a tainted-water problem in an aboriginal community that exposes a host of social problems). This is the most unfortunate way to get the media's attention.

People in the developing world are at a particular disadvantage when it comes to telling their stories. With a few exceptions, the main image of the developing world is that of war, famine, disaster and catastrophe. People in the world's poorer countries are powerless to change the way they are depicted in the North American media. This is where North American relief and development agencies can advocate on their behalf: telling the media that war and famine are not the only pictures of life in those places, that there is hope, too. You can help members of the media to meet people from those countries, either living in North America or in the developing world itself, so they can speak for themselves.

It is not enough to criticize the media for the way it portrays people in the world's poorer countries. It also has to be supplied with positive news from those places.

11. It's a way to be accountable

As a non-profit organization, you are accountable to the people who give you money, whether it be donations from individuals or organizations or government funds. A good way to show that you take this accountability seriously is to let donors and the general public know how you are using the money – showing the difference it is making in the lives of the people you serve. Since most people don't read your annual report, the easiest way to be accountable to them is by working with the media.

12. It's a way to improve media coverage

Many people complain about media coverage, but don't do anything to try to improve it. For example, people who complain that the media only gravitates to stories of crime and despair in North America's inner cities often don't try to tell reporters about the stories of hope. Reporters are usually open to telling the other side of the story. If they have reported erroneous information, they want to correct it. This is important, because once an erroneous bit of information gets into a media outlet's archive, it can be resurrected and repeated by future reporters, unless someone sends them a correction.

13. It's an aid to fundraising

A few years ago I helped a local business person obtain media coverage about his new small business. Later, when he went to the bank for a loan, his banker told him, "I read about you in the newspaper. I have the article in your file." He got the loan.

As it did for my businessman friend, good publicity can also help non-profit organizations raise money. Dollars won't pour in because you are on radio or TV or in the newspaper (unless it is about an emergency appeal of some kind). But when you go to ask people for money, you can show them newspaper clippings or refer to the coverage in your fundraising letters. Plus, if you are in the media frequently, people become familiar with your group. It makes obtaining support that much easier.

Who is the media?

By "media" we mean the people who work at daily and weekly newspapers, alternative newspapers or magazines, news and feature magazines, news departments at radio and TV stations, and wire services. To work with the media, you need to understand who they are and how they operate.

For the daily and weekly media, most reporters you will deal with are general assignment reporters. They are available to cover whatever stories come up that day. In the morning they may be covering a three-car accident downtown; in the afternoon they are interviewing you about the causes of famine in Africa; tomorrow it will be a story about tensions over gay ordination in a particular church.

Reporters who cover specific subjects (e.g., business, police/courts, city hall, sports) are called "beat" reporters. For issues that non-profits are involved in (e.g., international development, health, poverty, social justice, faith), there are almost no beat reporters, although there may be individual reporters who are interested in these subjects.

When it comes to radio or TV – morning, drive-home and call-in shows – you will usually not deal with the host but with a producer. He or she will do a pre-interview with you, then pass that information along to the host or on-air personality who will do the actual on-air interview.

Reporters do not make the decisions about which stories to publish or pursue, although they can make a case for a story to their editors. At larger daily newspapers, editors (e.g., local, foreign, feature, entertainment, sports, business, religion) make these decisions; at radio and TV stations it is news directors. TV and radio stations may also have story meetings, where reporters and producers pitch stories and the group votes on the ones it thinks are worth covering.

Cutbacks in the media over recent years mean fewer reporters are doing more and more work. As a result, each has less time to devote to any given story and probably has a number of stories on the go on any given day. Time for research is at a premium; reporters will greatly appreciate anything you can do to make getting the story easier.

Rules the media lives by

As with any other workplace, the media has rules to guide its activities. Knowing these rules will help you understand the mindset of a reporter who calls.

1. Reporters strive to be impartial

The media's greatest asset is the perception that it is neutral. This is different from saying that reporters are "objective" – that they have no personal opinion on an issue. Often, they do, but their task is to keep that opinion out of the story. They do this by making sure to report both sides of a story, thereby inviting the reader, viewer or listener to arrive at his or her own independent conclusion.

For example, if you are critical of a government policy, the reporter would note your point of view and then ask someone in the government for a response – someone who may refute your opinion or dispute your facts. Sometimes, it will be the other way around. The government might announce a new policy or initiative that affects your group and a reporter would call you for a response.

2. The media won't always take your word for it

You and your group are honest and truthful. You only want to tell it as it is. You especially want to make sure that the people and causes you advocate for are heard by the media. That's why sometimes you have to communicate your concerns about government policies that you feel will hurt the poor, denigrate the environment or impinge on religious freedoms. A reporter will dutifully record your comments, but will be obligated to contact a government spokesperson who can provide a rebuttal to your argument and tell the government's side of the story. The reporter has not done this to harm you, but rather to prevent the newspaper, radio or TV station from appearing to be one-sided and unbalanced. Again, that is part of being impartial, making sure that media consumers get both sides of an issue. A reporter may personally support the aims of your organization but he or she must, at all costs, avoid looking as if he or she is advocating for you or for your point of view. For the media, balance is important.

3. Media outlets assume that the public has a right to know

Reporters work on the assumption that the public has a right to know things about your organization. It is the reporter's job to get this information. This does not mean that reporters are constantly monitoring your group and its activities; there is far too much going on in the world, and far too few reporters, to do that. But when the situation arises, they will pursue a story about your group in the belief that the public has a right to know what you are doing. This is particularly true if your group is involved in issues that relate to public policy, if your group works with children (the public and the media are very alert and sensitive to issues of child abuse or endangerment), or if your group receives money from the public or the government.

4. Editors and reporters are interested in the local angle

The first axiom of reporting is that a car crash in your hometown is bigger news than a train wreck overseas, unless someone from your hometown was in the train wreck. In other words, the media wants to find ways to tie an event that happens far away to something local, because that is what people are most interested in. When reporters read a news release, they want to know how this will affect people in my community and whether anyone from the community is involved in the event or issue.

5. News organizations are interested in what is happening now

Reporters are not interested in things that have happened; they want to report about current events. An event that happened last week is not going to draw much media attention.

6. You have no control over the final product

A reporter will not let you read an article before publication, or hear or see a report before air time. Don't even think of asking. If you are not comfortable with this approach, don't agree to be interviewed.

A day in the life of a newspaper

To understand how the media works, let's walk in the footsteps of Alice, the city editor at a typical daily newspaper.

The day begins at about 8 a.m., when the first reporters and Alice straggle in. Alice sits down at her computer at the front of the newsroom and reads the messages the night editor has left. It turns out one of the stories filed by a reporter the day before has too many holes (missing information) to be published.

"Is it worth adding the information, or should we just let the story die?" the night editor asks.

The reporter who filed the story won't be in that day and another will have to do the work. Alice makes a mental note to take another look at it later in the day. Maybe a different angle can be developed to give the story a bit more staying power.

Alice looks around the newsroom at the reporters who are already there. Some are working at their computers; others are reading the newspaper.

"Time to get them going," she says to herself, reaching into a cabinet behind her desk and pulling out a folder with information on events taking place that day. There are dozens, more than the reporters will be able to handle. She sifts through news releases and reminders to determine which have real story potential and should be assigned. Some are passed on to the photo editor as possible "stand-alone" shots – photos with a caption but no story. The weakest news releases and story ideas are thrown out.

On a busy news day, assignments given early on may be eclipsed by more important ones. It is not unusual for a reporter to be working on a half-dozen stories at the same time. Generally it is the editor's job to tell the reporter which story has precedence.

Assignments are recorded alongside the reporters' names. At about 11:30 a.m., Alice grabs the list and heads into a meeting with other editors to co-ordinate efforts and share the news for tomorrow up to that point. In the meeting, story ideas are sharpened and some priorities are set.

By mid-afternoon, the pace in the newsroom accelerates. Alice checks with reporters to see how stories are shaping up. Reporters are grilled. Those working on potential page-one stories are given special attention. "What's the lead [the all-important first paragraph]? Who have you talked to? Make sure you talk to so-and-so. Make sure it is ready by five because it may have to be 'lawyered' for possible libel and slander. What information is missing?"

An assistant editor has arrived to help carry the load into the hectic early-evening hours. Alice briefs him on the stories in progress and they debate the pros and cons of some of the angles. Changes are agreed to and the assistant talks to the reporters affected.

Some stories work out and others don't. There is always pressure to produce high-quality stories for page one and the covers of the inside sections. However, page-one candidates may be relegated to inside pages when they don't measure up.

The story inherited from the night editor because of the gaps in information has been passed on to another reporter. Though it just about died the night before, it is now a strong page-one contender because of a new angle and a lot of polishing.

At 5:30 p.m. the assistant editor takes the list of stories and joins other senior editors for a final meeting to select the front-page stories. Local front-page story candidates are pitted against national and international stories. Is the story a good read? Is it important? Is it news? Is it a solid angle? Is there good "art" (pictures or graphics)? Will the competition be carrying the story?

Other stories are selected for pages inside the paper and the section covers. A news editor decides where these stories will run, the size of headline they will have, and how long they will be. A copy editor reads the stories for content, clarity, grammar and spelling. Lead paragraphs are polished and repolished. Other editors take the stories, boil them down to the length requested by the news editor and write the headline to specification. The final version, complete with headline, goes back to the news editor for a final read. It is then sent on to the composing room where the pages are assembled.

2

Making News

What is news?

Now that you know why you should work with the media and you understand a little about how it all works, what are you going to say? You need to talk about news. But what is news?

Broadly speaking, news is something that happens – a decision that is reached, a program that is begun, a person who is appointed, a meeting that will be held, food that will be shipped. The chief ingredient of news is action.

News is also the unusual – things that don't happen every day. As an editor of a Canadian newspaper observed, "Planes land and take off safely every day. We only cover the ones that crash." In other words, doing what you do all the time is not news, unless you do more of it, do it in a way that you haven't done before, do it for people that you haven't helped before or change the way you do it. Another take on this is the man-dog principle. When a dog bites a man, that's not news. But if a man bites a dog, that's front-page material.

One newspaper editor says he judges the quality of a news release by asking himself this question: "Does it tell my readers something they don't know about something they care about, or should care about?"

Developing a nose for news is essential for success with the media. When an interviewer asked public relations expert Fraser Seitel for a foolproof way to get a news release used, he replied, "The 'secret' to getting a news release used by a reporter is to have one irreducible ingredient – news. If your release contains real news of relevance to readers, reporters will gladly use it. Writing fluff rather than news is the novice's most common mistake."

Consider issuing a news release when your organization does the following:

- starts something
- does more of something
- does something for the first time
- marks an important anniversary*
- changes direction

- ends something
- does less of something
- does something for the last time
- receives an award
- responds in a new way.

* Note that anniversaries don't have the same attraction they used to have. Let media outlets know when your organization celebrates a 10-, 20-, 25- or 50-year anniversary (or more), but don't expect them to be all that excited about it.

The importance of timeliness

In real estate, the three most important assets of a piece of property are location, location and location. For news, it is timeliness, timeliness and timeliness.

Of course, it also helps if you have something interesting to say and know how to communicate it to the media. But in the news business, timing is everything. When editors and news directors receive a news release, one of the first questions they ask is, Is it happening now?

For the daily media, newsworthiness is determined by timeliness. Reporters are not interested in something that happened last week or even a few days ago. When your organization has a new initiative, don't wait a week to tell the media about it. They want to know about it the moment you sign on the dotted line, receive the money, move into the new building, start the new program or send the food. Wait a week, or even a few days, and it will become old news, and perhaps not be covered.

This can be a challenge for communicators at many organizations. It is often the case that your colleagues on the program side will want to wait until everything is perfect – when they know with absolute certainty that the new initiative or program is turning out exactly as they planned. That's great for programming, but it is lousy when dealing with the media; by the time all the bugs have been worked out, it is usually old news, and the media is not very interested in that.

This calls for negotiation. Your colleagues need to know and understand the constraints you work under, and you need to respect their desire for caution and certainty. Sometimes it is better to wait with some news until there are some tangible results (e.g., until after the first class graduates, the food is distributed or the first clients are served). There is nothing worse than making a big splash to initiate a new program only to have it fail; experiences like that will only make the media cautious the next time you want to announce a new program.

But your colleagues also need to know that every detail doesn't have to be perfect for the media to be interested in the story. When it is in the organization's best interests to get the news out now, some details may not be completely known. This is especially true when the organization's main need is for donations or other support from the public. Getting the word out when the program is new and exciting is essential for fundraising; few people want to give to something that has already happened.

Responding to events

Announcing news promptly is one aspect of timeliness. Responding to current issues and events is another. When an event or issue that your group is involved in makes the news, and you want to respond with an opinion piece in the newspaper, you must do so immediately. Waiting a week or two until the response has been vetted by all levels of the organization is not an option. Your response needs to be at the media outlet within a day or two; when it takes longer than that, other events may supersede it and the media is no longer interested in what you have to say.

For example, when new statistics are released about poverty, and your group is involved in helping poor people, do you have a point of view to share? If the news is about crime, do you have programs or resources that deal with alternative ways of responding to the problem? If there is a news item that is critical of international development, can you suggest ways for donors to be sure their contributions are used wisely?

One of the problems with the media's emphasis on timeliness is that sometimes your organization's schedule cannot match the urgency the media feels. For example, when an event about an issue your group is involved in occurs today, reporters will want to talk to you now, not tomorrow or the day after, when it is more convenient for you or your colleagues. Sometimes you have to drop your plans and go with the media's timetable.

The local angle

Most of your promotional work will be with the local media. Occasionally you will want to get the story national exposure, but the bulk of your efforts will be in trying to attract local media in your community. If you are going to be successful, you will need to understand the importance of the local angle.

For international development organizations, the idea of the local angle is easy to see. Take a flood in a developing country that kills hundreds and leaves tens of thousands homeless. What kind of coverage will it get in the media – one or two articles or mentions? (Maybe more, if there are good pictures.) Contrast this with a flood in Canada or the US that kills few people, if any, and leaves hundreds homeless. Coverage can run for pages in the newspaper or many minutes on TV or radio. Why the discrepancy? The local angle.

Hundreds of years ago, the English poet John Donne observed that "no man is an island"; we are all "a part of the main." He is right, of course, but the collective news judgment today amounts to a rejection of that poetic notion. When it comes to the media, the "main" extends as far as the reach of the local newspaper or TV and radio station, or to bonds of shared nationality – an idea some American foreign correspondents explored in the 1960s. They sarcastically created the Racial Equivalence Scale, which showed the minimum number of people from each country who had to die in an airplane crash before it was news in the US. (For example, one American was equal to 100 Czechs, who were equal to 43 people from France.)

An understanding of the importance of the local angle will save you a lot of grief when working with the media. It will help you and your colleagues understand why the local media isn't interested in, for example, a terrible famine in Sudan unless they can find a local connection. What the news organizations in your area want to know is this: How does that event far away affect the lives of people who read the newspaper or watch or listen to TV or radio news? Why should their readers, viewers or listeners care?

For this reason, reporters will usually look for a local connection to the story – a person with family in the stricken country, someone from close to home who is working there or local people raising money to help. Of course, when the event is big enough (defined by how many people die or how extensive the damage is), the media will be compelled to report about it. Even then they will look for local doorways into the story – doorways that your group may be able to provide for them.

The human interest angle

Human interest is another highly regarded angle for the media. This is because media consumers – you and I – like to read, hear and watch reports about other people and want to know how the big events of life affect people such as themselves. The closing of a factory is a business story, but it is also a people story. Each worker who lost a job has a story to tell.

The human interest angle is something to keep in mind when writing a news release. Instead of just writing about a famine that affects millions, can you tell the story of one person who is hungry in that country? Instead of sending out a news release that says a particular government policy will adversely affect the poor, can you write about someone who is poor who will suffer adverse consequences? Instead of saying your organization depends on volunteers, can you let a person who is volunteering explain why he or she does it?

Stories about big numbers especially need a human interest angle. When a report talks about hundreds of thousands of people or billions of dollars, it is hard for most people to grasp the ramifications. A story about one individual or what $100 means to a starving person, on the other hand, can help us understand the larger issue. Likewise, complicated stories need help. It is not easy to explain why a country is impoverished; a discussion about global debt, international market forces and trade imbalances usually won't attract attention. By introducing the reader to an average person who suffers the effects of these forces, you can talk about those important factors without losing the reader's attention by the second paragraph.

One reporter told me that she never writes about poverty without trying to tell the story of a poor person. When writing about inadequate housing, she focuses on someone who lives in a poorly constructed home. From the stories of these people she can expand the story to include poverty or housing in their neighbourhood, city, province or state – and perhaps even in the whole country. But the doorway to the story is always one person's story. Your news releases can reveal the humanity behind the big stories, making them more interesting for the media and for the people you are trying to reach.

The importance of regular contact

A major advertising agency says that ads should appear at least 10 times a year in magazines, and 15 times a year in newspapers, for readers to recognize and remember them. What is true for readers is true for editors and news directors: if you want them to remember your organization, they need to hear about you more than once or twice a year. Since the goal of contacting the media is to get editors and news directors to take note of your news releases, it is important that they recognize your letterhead or logo and come to know that seeing it means a good story suggestion has arrived.

This kind of recognition only comes through regular contact. Essentially, it is the building of trust between your organization and the media. It can take a long time, since the media are wary of all the special interest groups clamouring for their attention. But over months or years they can come to realize that news releases on your organization's letterhead can be trusted.

While there is no rule about what "regular" means, at the very least it means not sending out a release once or twice a year. It also means quickly replacing the person doing media relations at your organization – you should not let months go by without any communication to the media.

Contact is enhanced when it is done regularly by the same person. The media will come to know this person and ask for him or her by name. This person should be skilled at writing news releases, talking to reporters and thinking ahead about stories and story angles. As well, when someone is designated to do this task, it frees up other staff. He or she can take calls from reporters that might keep other staff from doing their work. Many times media inquiries don't have to go to the executive director or a program director. A media liaison who is generally familiar with the working of the organization can answer many questions.

Regular contact involves more than just sending out news releases. It also means calling reporters to pitch ideas or comment on stories, compliment them on promotions or inquire about job changes. You can invite them out for coffee or a meal for a less formal conversation; often the easiest place to meet is in the cafeteria at the media outlet, if it has one. In this way you can build relationships with reporters. Good relationships don't replace good story ideas, of course. You won't get much coverage without good stories. But requests for help with stories, feature reports, op-eds or columns can come because reporters, editors and news directors know you and know the kind of help you can provide.

Becoming known to members of the media takes time. It can take a year or two of regular contact by the same person before a news outlet will become familiar with your organization and come to see it as a trustworthy source of information. You'll know you have become that kind of organization when the media calls you – not just the other way around.

3

The News Release

A reporter I know once wrote that he was thinking of putting a sign on his desk that read, "Caution: News release crossing."

He went on to say that "herds of roadkill masquerading as news releases cross my desk every day," but that only a few catch his attention, making him stop and take a second look.

His experience is not unique. News organizations receive a torrent of news releases each day. If you want your news release to rise above the pack, you need to grab attention. To do that, you need to know a few things about news releases: what they can do, how to write them, when to send them and whom to send them to.

Purpose of the news release

The most common and effective way to contact the media is through a news release. A telephone call or e-mail is quicker and requires less effort, but a phone call can easily be forgotten and an e-mail can get lost in the in-box; a piece of paper has a better chance of being retained and remembered.

There are four things a news release can do.

1. Attract the media's attention

Everyone who works in media relations should have the experience of standing beside a fax machine in the newsroom of a daily newspaper or radio or TV station. If they did, they would appreciate just how difficult it is to get noticed when hundreds of news releases pour into the newsroom every day – not counting those that come by regular mail and e-mail! The sheer volume of news releases means that editors can give each one very little time – in some cases, 30 seconds is the maximum. If the editor is not sold on the story in that short amount of time, the news release is thrown away.

To help them in their task, editors employ a form of triage. They can quickly discard any news releases that come from far away (other states or provinces). News releases about events that have already occurred can go next; ditto those about routine happenings and events. What will make a news release stick is if it says something new, different or unusual.

Think of the news release in terms of selling something. Your product is the story. The currency is the editor's or news director's time. You must sell him or her on the idea of spending time on your story. To do this, you must grab his or her attention very quickly and then hold it.

2. Help reporters to get it right

One of the most common complaints about reporters is that they "never get it right." That is untrue, of course. They get it right most of the time. But reporters do make mistakes. Helping them to minimize errors is one of the goals of a news release. Having something on paper can help reporters spell names correctly and get dates, places and times right. It can also help ensure that the main point you are trying to make is accurately reported.

3. Give shape to the story

Most of the reporters you will deal with are general assignment reporters. For some of them, your news release will be the first time they will have ever heard of you or thought about your issue. As a result, they may not know where to begin when it comes to telling the story. Your news release can help give them some direction by suggesting an angle they can pursue. They may or may not follow your suggestions; sometimes a story can take on a life of its own, one that you may not have thought of. But at least you will have done your part to help the media find a way through what might be unfamiliar or complicated territory.

4.   Provide a contact person

This is one of the most important purposes of the news release. The news release is only the first step in telling a story. The second step is providing the name of someone reporters can talk to. Getting reporters to call and ask for an interview is the whole point of sending out a news release. News outlets are not going to use your news release verbatim (although some small weeklies may do so, or small bits of it might be put into an upcoming events calendar). Reporters want to talk to somebody, even if it is just to get them to say the same things as in the news release. Make sure this contact person is available to talk to reporters for a day or two after the news release is sent out.

Additionally, the news release can provide basic information about your organization and give general contact information (e.g., address, telephone and fax numbers, e-mail and website addresses).

How to write a news release

There are a few simple rules to follow when writing a news release – rules that will increase the chances that reporters will notice your event or announcement. (You will find examples of news releases at the end of this chapter.)

1.   Use letterhead

The name and logo of your organization are important communication tools, telling editors and reporters at a glance who the news release is coming from. Because major media outlets are inundated by news releases each day, editors need to be able to tell which ones to keep and which ones to recycle. When you maintain regular contact with the media, over time they will recognize your group's name and logo, and associate you with being a good source of news, with the result that your news release goes into the "keep" pile.

Your letterhead doesn't have to be fancy; it could simply show the name of your organization in a large, readable font, as long as it quickly says where the news release is coming from.

2.   Give the date

One definition of news is that it is current – it's happening now. By putting the date at the top, you tell the media when the news release was sent. If there is no date, a busy editor may overlook it when trying to determine which ones on the pile of news releases to follow up.

3.   Indicate when the news can be reported

It is traditional to put the words "For Immediate Release" after the date. It means that reporters may follow up the news release right away.

4.   Draw attention through the header

The person collecting the news releases from the fax machine or opening the envelopes will look at the letterhead and logo, date, header and first paragraph. If the news release doesn't catch his or her attention by then, it will likely go into the recycling bin. For this reason, your header needs to stand out, both visually and by what it says. Visually, you can draw attention to the header by using a large font (and a different style font) and by bolding it. In terms of what it says, you don't need to be especially creative, although a teaser or a play on words can be effective. Usually, it is sufficient to make sure that the header presents the essential information. The news releases at the end of the chapter give examples of various headers.

5.   Use a subhead

A subhead gives you an additional opportunity to provide some essential information right at the top of the news release. This is critical, considering the limited amount of time an editor has to give to your news release. The subhead can provide extra information, such as the time, date and location of your event, details about your speaker, and how much it costs to attend.

6.   Use a dateline

The dateline is simply the name of your community, in capital letters, followed by the your province or state (e.g., WINNIPEG, Man. –). Editors want to know whether the news release is coming from the area they serve. If it comes from another state or province, they will be less interested in it.

7.   Write an attention-grabbing lead

In the movie *Broadcast News,* a reporter played by Albert Brooks tries to tell another reporter, played by Holly Hunter, how much he loves her. When they meet, he talks first about how he enjoys working with her, how he admires her reporting and other work-related things before finally blurting out, "I love you!" After this he turns away and says in a self-deprecating tone, "How'd you like that? I buried the lead."

Never bury the lead. The essential information – the who, what, where, when, why and how – needs to be in your first paragraph, or in your first and second paragraphs.

8.   Fill out details in the body

Next comes the body. These paragraphs expand on the who, what, where, when, why and how of your news release. These paragraphs provide information that helps reporters flesh out a story by giving them some angles, letting them know whom they can interview and what those people will say, and providing some shape to the story.

9.   Indicate the end

To indicate the end of the body of the news release, you can put END or the number 30. (The latter comes from the days of Morse code; it signalled the end of the transmission.) Using the word END or the number 30 is especially important when you send your news release by fax, so it is clear there are no more pages coming. This comes above the contact information, which is the information that appears at the bottom of the press release.

10. Include contact information

The purpose of sending the news release is to get reporters to call you and do an interview. For this reason, make sure to tell them whom to contact and how. The contact information goes after the end of the body of the press release; by bolding it, you can make sure that it is easy to see.

Tips on writing a news release

1. Keep it short

A news release should be one or two pages in length, with double spaced or 1.5 spaced print. If you can keep it to one page, all the better.

2. Avoid jargon

Every non-profit organization uses in-house language – words, phrases and acronyms that those in the organization understand, but that confuse people outside of it. If you aren't sure whether your news release contains jargon, ask your mother or a friend to read it. If they become confused, take another look at the wording.

3. Explain acronyms

Acronyms are handy: they help you save space in a news release. In the international development world, common acronyms include NGO, CIDA, PVO, ODA and USAID. To outsiders, these acronyms are meaningless. In instances when you do not want to repeat a long organization name or title, write it out on first reference, with the acronym immediately following in parentheses. Then you can use the acronym throughout the rest of the text. Example: "Non-governmental organizations (NGOs) are widely acclaimed as being among the most efficient ways of providing overseas development assistance."

4. Avoid exclusive language

Words such as "brotherhood," "businessman," "policeman" or "spokesman" leave out half the population. Instead, use inclusive terms such as "community," "business person," "police officer" or "spokesperson."

5. Eschew obfuscation

Avoid using hard-to-understand words. As George Orwell suggested, don't use a big word when a short one will do, and don't use a three-syllable word when a one-syllable word will do.

6. Try to highlight people

Organizations and organizational activity can be boring. The process of reaching an important decision is rarely very dramatic. Program activity often involves meetings, sitting at a desk, and talking on the phone. That is why it is best to highlight people in your news releases. Instead of talking about a program that provides services for inner-city parents, tell the story of parents who have benefited from the service. Instead of talking about how much food was given for a feeding program, highlight some of the donors. These people can open doors into the story, making it much more interesting and attractive to reporters.

7. Keep it simple

While a news release needs to be well written, it does not have to be great literature. You are not trying to write a piece of art that overflows with nuance, metaphor and imagery. The words you write will most likely not be published verbatim by the newspaper or repeated by the news announcer or reporter. You are providing the media with a skeleton of basic facts; the reporter will put flesh on the bones.

Sending a news release

1. To whom?

After a non-profit organization in Winnipeg received some favourable media attention on a local radio station, I complimented its public relations person on a job well done. "It was easy," she replied. "I know someone at the station."

I didn't say it, but I thought, "If that's how you get on that station, you had better hope the person you know never leaves."

Effective media relations does not depend on knowing people in the media. Your success is determined by the quality of the stories you provide, not by whom you know. Knowing people in the media can help, and over time you will get to know various reporters and editors. But even a reporter who is your best friend will not be able to persuade his or her editors to cover your events if you don't have good stories.

In fact, sometimes depending on knowing someone at a media outlet can *hurt* your chances of getting attention. Say you are in the habit of addressing your news release to an individual you know at a TV station or newspaper (as opposed to the news director or city desk). When this individual goes on vacation, the letter or fax can sit unnoticed on his or her desk for days or weeks, or the e-mail can sit unopened in the inbox.

It is always better to send your news releases to the news director at a TV or radio station, or to one of the various desks or editors at a newspaper (e.g., city desk, business, entertainment or religion editor). A large daily newspaper may have one city editor and several assistant editors. You may not know which one is working the desk that day or that morning. Addressing the letter or fax to "City Editor" will get it to the right place, regardless of who is there. You can also send a copy to a reporter who has a special interest in your issue or group. Over time you may get to know a specific reporter who wants to be updated on a certain issue; then it is fine to address things to him or her.

It used to be that if you wanted contact information for newspapers across North America, you had to use a printed directory. Today, however, you can go to the Internet for this information. To find contact information, go the media outlet's website: most now provide names and contact information for their staff. If you don't know the media outlet's website address, use a search engine or one of many websites that list media outlets around the world.

2. How?

There was a time when most news releases were sent by mail. Next came the fax machine. Now there is e-mail, which makes sending a news release easy. But e-mail may not always be the best way to communicate with the media. Why? Because they receive so much of it. In my opinion, the best way to send a news release is still by fax. The media outlet gets an actual piece of paper that someone has to handle. Plus, it saves a step or two, since no one has to print it and file it.

That said, you can use e-mail to communicate with individual reporters. As you deal with them, you will discover which ones prefer to use this medium – who reads their messages and responds. Once you have established this relationship, it is fine to use e-mail to deal with them. Be careful about sending attachments, though. With so many viruses around, people are rightfully wary of opening attachments from people they don't know. Also pay attention to your subject line; some spam blockers will automatically quarantine e-mails that use words frequently found in spam (e.g., "free" or "money").

3. To which media outlets?

News releases should be sent to all media outlets in the local viewing, listening and reading area. Why? Because the people you want to reach don't get all their information from one source. If everyone tuned into the same TV station or read the same newspaper, you could send your news releases to just one or two media outlets. But people get their information from many media sources, including types you may not prefer. Don't let your personal prejudices guide your decisions. By excluding one source or another (e.g., a tabloid newspaper) you limit the number of people your message will reach.

Another reason for sending releases to all outlets is that you don't want to play media favourites. Don't get in the habit of sending news tips to only one media outlet (because you know the reporter, for instance). This may get you coverage by that media outlet, but could cost you broader coverage by the others in the future. You want everyone to want your story.

What about newspapers? With so much attention being given today to the electronic media, it is easy to think that the days of reading are over. But there is still a good reason to send your news releases to newspapers. Although TV is the preferred source of news for 63 per cent of Canadians, and approximately 13 per cent get their news from the radio, the total daily circulation of Canada's 102 daily newspapers was about five million copies in 2002, meaning that each day about one in five adult Canadians received a daily newspaper, one of the highest ratios in the world. (A 2002 survey found that local news had the highest readership, at 73 per cent, followed by world news at 65 per cent, provincial and national news at 60 per cent, arts and entertainment at 44 per cent, sports at 36 per cent and editorials at 30 per cent.) Meanwhile, 71 per cent of English-speaking Canadians read one of Canada's 706 community newspapers at least once a month. (Only seven per cent of Canadians rely primarily on the Internet for accurate news and information.)

The daily newspaper is also your doorway to coverage by TV and radio. One of the first thing TV news directors and radio hosts do when they come to work is read several newspapers, both local and national. TV and radio stations that have reporters use newspapers as cues for which stories to cover that day. Radio stations that don't have reporters, but have a short newscast at the top of each hour, use newspapers to create their newscasts. This is why things you read in the newspaper sometimes turn up on the radio, repeated almost word for word; print journalists derisively refer to this practice as "rip and read."

Finally, although the people who read newspapers are older than those who turn to broadcast or electronic sources for their news, they have more disposable income to give to non-profit organizations such as yours. You don't want to miss any opportunity to reach out to potential supporters.

Remember to include the various newspaper wire services on your mailing and fax lists. In today's world of fibre optics and computers, the term "wire service" is out of date; the words don't move by wire as they used to. But the term is still in use for services such as Canadian Press (CP), Associated Press (AP) and United Press International (UPI) in the US, and Reuters international.

Wire services are organized into city, state and provincial bureaus. The bureaus do two things: generate stories about their coverage areas and abridge articles from local daily papers to place on the "wire" and send to member media outlets across the country or around the world. Major media outlets have editors who scan the "wires" on a regular basis to see what stories are coming across. A story about your organization that is picked up by a wire service may appear in newspapers or be reported by radio stations across the country.

4.   When and how many?

Send out a news release as early in the day as possible, when the media is hungriest for story ideas. If you want to get something into the next morning's paper, send the news release out before noon; most morning papers have late afternoon deadlines. The same holds true when you want to get something on the evening TV news. A mid-morning or midday event gives the reporter enough time to prepare.

Times of the week to avoid are late Friday afternoon and weekends. Morning and drive-home radio shows don't broadcast on weekends; local TV stations often don't have supper-hour newscasts on weekends; all media sources operate with fewer reporters. They simply aren't as able to respond to news on weekends the way they can during the week (which is precisely why organizations release their bad news late on Friday afternoons). When you must send something then, make sure someone from your organization is willing to be contacted at home by a reporter. When the information can wait, send it first thing Monday morning; more media outlets will be able to respond to your release.

For an event that is planned for a long time from now, send your news release two weeks before the event occurs. Media outlets that decide to keep the news release will put it into a file (sometimes called a "1 to 30 file") that is organized by the days of the month. On the week that your event occurs, the assignment editor will go to the file and see what is happening that week. On Monday morning of the week of the event, send another news release as a reminder and follow up with a phone call to make sure the news release arrived. You could send another reminder the day before the event, just to be sure.

Three news releases is the maximum. Don't do what the local Earth Day committee in my city did a few years ago, when it sent news releases to every reporter at every media outlet. Not surprisingly, one of the questions reporters asked was, "Since Earth Day is about preserving the environment, how can you justify using so much paper to let the media know about the event?" The spokespeople were embarrassed, needless to say.

5.   When not to send a news release

Sometimes the best course of action is *not* to send a news release. Here is an example: You have been preparing for weeks for the launch of a new program. You have set the date and time for a news conference. Then the river in your city overflows its banks, a major local personality dies or a war breaks out. When that happens, it is best to postpone the release of your news. Wait a bit; reporters will soon tire of reporting exclusively about even the most gripping of events and will become hungry for something else, especially if it is a bit of good news to lighten a load of bad news.

Examples of news releases

Below are examples of news releases I have sent out about events. They will give you some ideas for structure, format and content.

EXAMPLE 1

This news release not only tells what, when, where and how much, it talks about why it is important for people to attend the workshop and why this church is putting it on. It provides reporters with a couple of angles.

RIVER EAST MENNONITE BRETHREN CHURCH

755 McLeod Ave., Winnipeg, Man. 663-5096

HEALTHY WAYS TO DEAL WITH FAMILY, WORKPLACE CONFLICTS FOCUS OF FALL WORKSHOPS

Workshops offered by the River East Mennonite Brethren Church, 755 McLeod Ave.; first session to be held September 25.

WINNIPEG, Man. – What do you do when your children drive you crazy? How can you deal with that irritating co-worker? What about those neighbours who play their music too loud late at night?

These conflicts can make our lives miserable. Fortunately, there are ways to deal with them, ways that can help us find peaceful resolutions that preserve our relationships at work, at home and in our neighbourhood.

Helping people find healthy ways to deal with conflict is the focus of a three-session workshop being offered by the River East Mennonite Brethren Church, 755 McLeod Ave. The sessions run Wednesday evenings from 7 to 9 p.m., beginning September 25 and continuing October 2 and October 9. The presenter is Jan Schmidt, the former director of Winnipeg's Mediation Services, who is currently involved in workplace intervention programs. Cost for all three sessions is $5.

The first session will focus on understanding conflict; the second will look at ways to unravel misunderstandings and disagreements; and the last will offer pathways to conflict resolution.

Childcare is available, but children must be preregistered, at a cost of $2 per child per session.

According to River East Pastor Connie Epp, the workshops are being offered as a way for the church to provide "practical resources for the entire community" and not simply be "a place that is only open on Sunday mornings for a select few."

"It's also a way to show that if we want a peaceful world, we need to start in our own backyard, through our family and workplace relationships," she says.

The sessions are part of River East's Wellness Workshop series. Another series on parenting will be offered in January 2003, with a third series on self-understanding in April.

- 30 -

For more information or to register for the conflict resolution sessions, call the church at XXX-XXXX.

Example 2

Nothing special about this news release: it just presents the who, what, where, why, when and how much it will cost. As a bonus, it is short enough to be used as a public service announcement.

Winnipeg Model Railroad Club

**Meeting at Christ Church Anglican, 1735 Corydon
on the second Friday of each month, Sept. to April**

September 4, 2002
For Immediate Release

"ALL ABOARD!" FOR RAILROAD FUN AT ANNUAL GREAT CANADIAN TRAIN SHOW

**Thomas the Tank Engine layout to be featured
at Sept. 21–22 show to benefit Children's Hospital**

WINNIPEG, Man. – It's "All aboard!" for railroad fun at the annual Great Canadian Train Show and Flea Market, to be held September 21–22 at the Mennonite Brethren Collegiate Institute, 180 Riverton Ave. (near the corner of Talbot and Disraeli).

The show will feature operating layouts, displays of model buildings and a sale of used model railroad items. A special feature at this year's show will be the appearance of Thomas the Tank Engine on a 4- by 6-foot layout of the mythical Isle of Sodor.

Proceeds from the show will be used to support the Children's Hospital.

Times for the show are 10 a.m. to 5 p.m. on Saturday, Sept. 21, and 11 a.m. to 4 p.m. on Sunday, Sept. 22. Admission is $3 per person or $6 for a family.

The Winnipeg Model Railroad Club was founded in 1955 with the aim of enabling Winnipeggers to enjoy and grow in the hobby of model railroading.

- 30 -

For more information or to arrange to visit a home model railroad layout, contact John Longhurst at XXX-XXXX.

EXAMPLE 3

This news release is about a big issue and some big names who will be speaking about it. It asks a question and invites the media to come and learn some answers.

FAITH *and the* MEDIA

January 2, 2002
For Immediate Release

MEDIA COVERAGE OF FAITH AFTER 9/11 SUBJECT OF JANUARY 21 COMMUNITY FORUM

Local and national media and faith group representatives to address question "Has the media done a better or worse job of covering faith since September 11?"

WINNIPEG, Man. – Before September 11, coverage of faith by the media was mostly confined to the faith page of newspapers or occasional reports by the broadcast media about the very weird or the very inspirational. Subsequently, however, it is rare not to hear something about religion – in this case, Islam – every day in the media.

Should we have had to wait for the terrible terrorist attacks to see more reporting about Islam in the media? How has the media done in its coverage of this religion since September 11? What about coverage of other religions since that time? And how have faith groups done when it comes to helping the media understand religion? **These are some of the questions to be addressed at the Faith and the Media Community Forum, January 21, 7–9 p.m. at Jubilee Place, 180 Riverton Avenue (at Mennonite Brethren Collegiate Institute, near the corner of Talbot and Disraeli).**

Panelists at the forum are **Nick Hirst**, Editor, Winnipeg Free Press; **Kirk LaPointe**, Senior Vice-President, CTV News; **Gord Legge**, Director, Centre for Faith and the Media; and **Riad Saloojee**, Executive Director of the Council on American-Islamic Relations–Canada. The moderator is **Donald Benham**, CBC Radio One. The forum will include time for audience participation and questions.

The forum is sponsored by the Department of Canadian Heritage. Admission is free.

Refreshments to follow.

- 30 -

For more information, call XXX-XXXX or XXX-XXXX.

EXAMPLE 4

Finding people who are willing to talk about personal experiences is an important way to get the media's attention. This couple was also willing to be interviewed before the event to help generate publicity, so that more people might come.

March 24, 1994
For Immediate Release

VICTIMS OF CRIME TO TALK ABOUT HOW CRIME HURTS, JUSTICE HEALS AT WEEKEND CONFERENCE

Parents of teenager killed by hit-and-run driver to share Friday evening, 7:30 p.m., at Fort Garry Evangelical Mennonite Church, 602 Pasadena.

WINNIPEG, Man. – Eight months ago, tragedy struck Mark and Mabel Smith when their teenage son was killed by a hit-and-run driver.

Today, after the court case that found the driver guilty of careless driving, the Smiths want to meet the young man to tell him they forgive him.

"Nothing can change the situation. Our son will never come back," says Mark. "But we need to set ourselves and the driver free to get on with our lives."

The Smiths will be sharing the story of their experience with crime this weekend at the Mennonite Central Committee (MCC)–sponsored conference called Crime Hurts, Justice Heals: Christians Responding to Crime. The conference will take place March 25 and 26 at the Fort Garry Evangelical Mennonite Church, 602 Pasadena. The Friday session begins at 7:30 p.m.; the Saturday session goes from 9:00 a.m. to 4:00 p.m.

Also talking about experiences with crime will be Elaine Egan, whose home was broken into and set afire, and Wilma Derksen, whose daughter Candace was murdered in 1985.

Egan chose to work through her emotions by participating in Face-to-Face, an MCC program that brings victims of break-and-enter together with jailed offenders convicted of that crime. Derksen is widely known for her book about how she was able to forgive her daughter's murderer.

Feature speaker at the conference is Dave Worth of Kitchener, Ont., who helped develop one of the first mediation services programs in North America. Topics to be discussed include biblical perspectives on crime and justice and understanding the impact of crime. Workshops on domestic violence and restorative justice, mediation for young offenders and conflict resolution in schools will also be offered.

Cost of the conference is $15 per person ($10 for students and unemployed).

MCC is the relief and development arm of the North American Mennonite and Brethren in Christ Churches. There are around 1,000 MCC workers serving in 55 countries, including the US and Canada.

- 30 -

For more information, contact John Longhurst, XXX-XXXX.

EXAMPLE 5

Anniversaries, in and of themselves, are not of great interest to the media. How can you get reporters interested? Tell stories of the people who have benefited from the organization.

February 25, 1994
For Immediate Release

LOAN FUND FOR INNER-CITY BUSINESSES MARKS SUCCESSFUL FIRST YEAR OF OPERATION

Native casket company among 16 businesses started or helped by SEED Winnipeg

WINNIPEG, Man. – Carl Smith of Winnipeg had a good idea for a new business. The ex-biker also had no steady job, no collateral and a spider tattoo on the side of his face, hardly a combination that would inspire a bank to take a chance on a loan.

Today, however, the father of five has seen his dream come true with help from SEED Winnipeg, a Mennonite Central Committee (MCC) Manitoba–sponsored organization that loans money to low-income residents who want to start their own businesses. Smith is owner of ABC Caskets, a company that makes coffin liners that add cultural significance and dignity to aboriginal funerals.

"SEED Winnipeg was incredibly helpful," says Smith, noting that the organization accepted his Harley-Davidson motorcycle as collateral. "I wouldn't have got this far without them," he adds.

ABC Caskets is just one of 16 businesses in Winnipeg that have begun, been stabilized or expanded during SEED Winnipeg's first year of operation. "We think we've made a very positive impact during our first year," says Garry Loewen, an MCC Manitoba staff person who was seconded to SEED Winnipeg to serve as its general manager.

To date, SEED Winnipeg has loaned $66,750. Funding for the loans comes from the Assiniboine and Crosstown credit unions, each of which has made $100,000 available to the organization. To be eligible for loans, which are offered at a rate of prime plus two per cent, applicants must have low incomes and be willing to work with SEED Winnipeg staff to prepare a business plan. Loans have ranged in size from $350 to $10,000; cost per job created or maintained is estimated to be around $3,500.

Other businesses and individuals assisted by SEED Winnipeg include a travel shop, a Latin American food store, a self-employed courier, a jeweller, a candle maker, an Aboriginal artist and a clothing designer, among others.

"There's a lot of interest in what we do," says Loewen. "People are excited to get a chance to get off welfare to put their dreams into action. But poor people typically do not have access to friends or family who can lend them money, and often they can't get funds from traditional sources like banks. We're willing to take a risk on them," he adds, noting that repayment on loans to date "has been heartening."

"There are a lot of side benefits to what we do that goes beyond job creation," he adds. "People who get started in business experience significant growth in self-esteem and they often become powerful role models for their families and community."

In addition to loaning money and helping with a business plan, SEED Winnipeg provides a mentor from the business community, offers support and encouragement, and links entrepreneurs with other sources of funding. In Smith's case, SEED Winnipeg worked with the federal government's Aboriginal Business Development Program, which gave him a grant for start-up costs.

In addition to MCC and the two credit unions, SEED Winnipeg is supported by a City of Winnipeg–funded inner-city agency, the province of Manitoba, Mennonite Economic Development Associates, Winnipeg Jewish Community Services Council, and a local foundation.

MCC is the relief and development arm of the North American Mennonite and Brethren in Christ churches. There are around 1,000 MCC workers serving in 55 countries, including the US and Canada.

- 30 -

For more information, contact Garry Loewen, XXX-XXXX

EXAMPLE 6

Often the doorway to a big issue is through a compelling personal story. This release tries to get at the issue of fair wages for workers in the developing world by starting with a couple that wanted to spend more when they buy things. At the same time, it publicizes an event related to the big issue.

February 8, 1995
For Immediate Release

WINNIPEG COUPLE LOOKING FOR WAYS TO SPEND MORE MONEY WHEN THEY SHOP

Smiths will be shopping at Alternative Trade Fair, Feb. 10–11 at Crossways in the Common

WINNIPEG, Man. – At a time when most Winnipeggers are looking for ways to save money when they shop, Joe and Joan Smith want to pay more for the things they buy.

The Smiths haven't lost their minds. They're just willing to pay a bit more for items that are environmentally safe and produced by workers who receive a fair wage for their labour. "We estimate it costs us around 10 to 15 per cent more a year to be socially conscious shoppers," says Joe.

The Smiths will be doing some shopping this weekend at the Alternative Trade Fair, an event that brings together organizations that sell products from the developing world and provide fair wages to workers. The fair will be held Friday, Feb. 10, 7–10 p.m., and Saturday, Feb. 11, noon to 10 p.m. at Crossways in the Common at Broadway and Furby Street.

The fair will feature the sale of crafts from overseas communities, a coffee house and live music by musicians from Chile, Mexico, the Andes and Canada.

Joe admits it is hard to tell which companies pay their workers wages of $2 to $3 dollars a day for products that sell for $40 to $50 each in Canada. But when they find companies that provide fair wages, they buy these products, even if they cost more.

"We had committed ourselves to giving ten per cent of our income to overseas development work," he says. "But this is a better way to help people overseas by making sure that people have good paying jobs so they can support themselves and their families."

Stores and agencies that promote products made by companies that pay fair wages to workers are called Alternative Trading Organizations (ATOs). ATOs in Winnipeg include the Mennonite Central Committee–supported SELFHELP Crafts of the World, the Olive Branch Gift Shop, CUSO and Oxfam. They provide artisans and business people in the developing world with access to North American markets and make sure they receive full value for their labour.

"We provide a commercial outlet for artists and craftspeople overseas who are too small to attract large North American business chains," says Jackie Roe of SELFHELP Crafts of the World. "By selling their products we give them an opportunity to support themselves and their families, which is a lot better than sending them relief aid."

As well as providing a fair wage and access to markets, ATOs enable people in rural areas in the developing world to stay in their home communities, instead of having to move to overcrowded cities. "Instead of living in a slum and eking out a living in an unhealthy sweatshop, they can stay home and preserve their families and their local culture."

Examples of products that will be sold at the fair include woodcarvings, baskets, textiles, jewellery, hand-woven silks and cottons, greeting cards, toys and candle holders. Some stores also sell food, such as coffee, tea, wild honey, cocoa, and wild rice processed by Aboriginal people in northwestern Ontario.

By coming to the fair, Winnipeggers who are concerned about exploitation of factory workers in the developing world "can have the satisfaction of knowing that the makers of these products are properly compensated," Joe says.

The fair is sponsored by CUSO, the Marquis Project in Brandon, Tools for Peace, Olive Branch, SELFHELP Crafts of the World and the Manitoba League of the Physically Handicapped.

- 30 -

For more information, call Joe Smith at XXX-XXXX at home or XXX-XXXX at work.

4

The Interview

S uccess! Media outlets have received your news release and reporters want to talk to you for a story. Now what?

Who will interview you?

Most of the reporters who will interview you will be general assignment reporters, unless the media outlet has a beat reporter assigned to
your issue (e.g., health, religion, environment). In other words, these
reporters may know very little about your issue; all they will have to
go on will be the news release you have sent them. Keep this in mind
during the interview. Don't assume they know where Malawi is, what
the symptoms of Type 2 diabetes are or how a Southern Baptist is different from someone from the North American Baptist Conference. If
you think a reporter is having trouble keeping it all straight, offer to
fax or e-mail him or her a fact sheet or provide the address for your
website.

For some radio shows, you will first be interviewed by a producer,
although occasionally you may hear directly from the host. During
this pre-interview, the producer will determine whether you have
a good story to tell and whether you are able to tell it well on radio
(e.g., you speak clearly with a minimum of "ums" and "uhs," you do
not have an accent that is hard to understand, you are not timid and
uncertain). If the interview is to go ahead, the producer will pass the

information you shared on to the host, who can then look incredibly smart and knowledgeable when he or she asks perceptive and informative questions.

In other words, the purpose of this pre-interview is to determine whether you should go on air or not. In some cases, you won't even know that this is what is happening. A number of years ago, I received a call from Mary Lou Findlay, who was at that time the host of a CBC radio show about the media. She called me up out of the blue to say she was doing a show on how the media covers religion and asked my thoughts on the subject. We had a wide-ranging 20-minute discussion on the topic, at the end of which she asked, "Would you be willing to participate in a panel on the subject for the show?" I said I would.

But the conversation could just as easily have gone the other way. At the end, Findlay could have simply said thanks and goodbye. She didn't because she decided that what I had to say was sufficiently interesting and different from what other guests were prepared to share. Plus, she judged that I was able to speak on radio: I didn't speak too quickly, wasn't hard to understand, and didn't say "um" a lot.

How will you be interviewed?

For most newspaper stories, you will be interviewed over the phone; it saves the reporter time. When the story is more in-depth, or there are a number of people to interview, the reporter may come and talk to you in person. You will never be asked to go to a newsroom to be interviewed. When a photograph is needed, a photographer will be sent out later (the reporter at a daily paper usually does not take photos, but a reporter for a weekly or monthly paper often does both). When the newspaper intends to run just a photo and a caption, you will not be interviewed at all. You'll just have your photo taken and the newspaper will use information from your news release.

Radio stations prefer that you come in to be interviewed if you have been invited onto a show; they get much better sound quality that way.

Radio hosts may want to interview you over the phone. Stations that have reporters will interview you for a news report at your office or at the site of an event, using recording equipment.

When there is some action to show, a TV reporter will come to interview you. TV reporters usually like to avoid showing too many talking heads, although you may occasionally be interviewed in that manner when you can provide a local perspective on a national or international event or when they have footage they can run with your comments.

What should you say?

The most important thing to remember about being interviewed is that everything is on the record – it can appear in the newspaper or be used in a radio or TV report – from the moment the reporter introduces himself or herself. Few reporters will formally say "May I interview you?" to obtain permission to quote you. By merely identifying themselves as reporters they believe you have been sufficiently warned that everything you say can be quoted. Remember this and you will not find things you never meant to be quoted about in the newspaper! (This approach can pose some problems if you have established a relationship with the reporter. Is he or she just calling to chat, get some background information, or are you going to be quoted? When in doubt, ask.)

If you are taped for TV, it should be obvious that you are being interviewed; you are looking at a camera, after all. Radio is similar, even over the phone; the radio reporter will ask to record your comments (he or she will ask a question, then there will be silence on the other end as you answer). In both cases, however, a reporter could call you up for comments and then quote you on air.

You can ask to go "off the record" when talking to a reporter, although many reporters will resist this request. After all, how can they do their job if they can't get any quotes? If you are asked a question that you cannot answer for some reason, say so. You could say, "I don't have enough information to comment on that," or "I'm not qualified to respond to that question." The reporter may then want to know when you will be able to get the information or who in your organization is qualified to speak on the matter. When that happens, indicate when you or someone else will be able to respond. The worst thing you can do is try to make up an answer on the spot. You don't want to be responsible for sharing incorrect information with the public via the media.

Other times, the question may be about something that you are not free to comment on – a personnel matter or something that affects the privacy of staff or clients, for example. When this happens, don't just say, "No comment." Those words have come to mean "Something terrible is going on, and I have to make sure I hide it from view," and may only make the reporter press even harder for an answer. Rather than risk seeing the issue blown out of proportion, say that you cannot comment and tell the reporter why.

For example, in the late 1980s a relief organization I worked for operated in Eritrea, which at the time was involved in a civil war with Ethiopia. The agency had workers in that country, as well as in Ethiopia. To protect the workers in Ethiopia from expulsion, we made a point of referring to relief efforts in Eritrea as occurring in "northern Ethiopia." We did this because the Ethiopian government still saw the breakaway province as part of Ethiopia and suggested that any references to it as a separate nation might lead to consequences for foreign relief workers. An off-the-record conversation with a reporter let him know why we could not indicate exactly where food relief was going.

This technique also works for taped radio and TV interviews. There is nothing wrong with saying you are unable to answer a question for the reasons given above. When necessary, ask for the tape recorder or TV camera to be turned off so you can explain yourself, and then resume the interview.

When you are on live radio or TV, you cannot go off the record or stop the interview, but you can respond in ways that allow you to acknowledge the question. Resist the urge to speculate about the motives of others; stick to what you know best. Here is an example:

- *Some people say that we shouldn't send outdated medical supplies to poor countries.* "That's a big concern, but my organization doesn't send medical supplies overseas. What we focus on is...."

- *It seems to me that the biggest issue facing poor people in Canada is the low minimum wage. What about that?* "The issue of poverty has many important aspects, but the one that my organization deals with is...."

- *Why do you think the minister won't make more money available for these programs?* "I don't know why she says that, but I know that money donated by people in this community can make a difference by...."

Another thing you want to avoid is commenting on the practices of other groups. You may believe that agency X has a terrible record when it comes to delivering relief supplies to starving people, but you don't want the media to quote you saying that. This happened to me once during a call-in show, when a caller vented his anger about another relief agency's practices. I shared his concern, but declined to join him in denouncing that agency. There is no benefit to having groups criticize each other publicly. Instead, I focused on how my agency sought to do its work.

The problem is less that a hard-nosed reporter squeezes information out of reluctant interviewees than more that people say too much to reporters. In addition to working in media relations, I have also worked as a reporter. I have found that the people I interview are sometimes so eager to talk about themselves or the group they work for that they reveal more than is appropriate. If I printed everything they told me, it would embarrass them and the group they represent. Many people have little experience with the media; the idea that they will be covered causes them to let their guard down temporarily, with the result that they say too much. They can also be so thrilled to be interviewed that they go to unusual lengths to be helpful, sometimes telling more than they should. If you find this happening to you, resist the urge.

An old axiom puts it this way: "Few people are misquoted. They're just horrified to see what they said in print."

Interview tips

Plan ahead

If you have some time to prepare for an interview, think of one or two main points that you want to make, and of some clear, crisp ways to present them. If you are preparing for a radio interview, it is fine to make some notes to remember your main points, but don't write a statement to read on air. One radio show host, confronted by a guest who began to read a prepared statement, interrupted the interview and deftly reached over to take away the piece of paper. It seemed cruel at the time, but he wanted to talk to a real person, not hear an official statement.

Take your time

When a reporter calls unexpectedly and asks a question you cannot answer on the spot, you don't have to answer immediately. When you need time to get information or organize your thoughts (particularly for a recorded radio interview), tell the reporter you will call back shortly. Always call back at the time you have indicated.

Assume the reporter knows little about your work or the issue you are involved in

Unless you are talking to a beat reporter, try to give as much background information as possible. One way to do this is to offer to fax or e-mail facts and figures when the interview is over, or to give the reporter the address for your group's website.

Spell names and places

Spell your name, particularly if it is difficult to pronounce. This helps ensure accuracy. If you are speaking about religious denominations, make sure to give the full and correct name, not the shorthand version everyone in the denomination uses (e.g., The Canadian Conference of Mennonite Brethren Churches, not "The MB Church"). The reporter will use whatever you say: after all, you're the expert.

Keep your comments short and to the point

This is especially true for radio and TV, where the sound bite rules. By self-editing your comments, you eliminate the need for the media to edit you, helping ensure that your points are made. Avoid long, rambling introductions to answers.

Expect mistakes

Mistakes are part of life; you make them, and so do reporters. The media strives to get it right, but errors inevitably occur. Often the mistakes are not the kind that the article turns on, such as the spelling of a name or place. The main point of the report is not lost because of a spelling error or because the report placed a village in the western part of Sudan when it is really in the east. These things may be irritating, but the average person likely won't notice or care about them. Decide which mistakes are worth correcting and which ones don't really matter before addressing them (see "What to do when the media gets it wrong" on page 105).

Be able to describe your organization in a few words

This is what is known as a "tag line." It has been said that when you cannot write the main purpose of your organization on the back of a business card, you won't be able to communicate successfully about it to people who are unfamiliar with it. You usually have only a few seconds or sentences to describe what your organization is about. Know your tag line.

Avoid jargon

We all use in-house language to describe ourselves, our partners and our activities. A sentence such as "MCC is one of the NGOs working in an LDC with other PVOs that are also doing R & D programs with funding from CIDA and USAID" makes sense to people involved in relief and development work, but is gobbledygook to anyone else. Don't speak this way to reporters.

Turn the interview in your direction

Sometimes reporters will call about a major issue that is dominating the media, but about which your group has nothing to say. Rather than just say nothing, you might be able to turn the interview in your direction. For example, if the reporter is calling about an earthquake in Iran, but your group has no contacts or program there, you could note that while your group isn't there it is involved in disaster relief in other countries that are no longer in the news but that still have real needs. If you can't make any connections to the story, help the reporter by giving contact information for other groups that might be involved in the issue at hand. ("We aren't involved in Iran, but CARE is. Do you want a phone number for their media relations person?")

Feel free to ask the reporter some questions

An interview is a two-way conversation. You can also ask the reporter questions. Key questions might include the following: "What's your deadline?" "What is the focus or angle of your story?" "What do you know about our organization?"

5

News Conferences
and Media Events

Sometimes you want to get the media to attend a news conference. Other times, you want to invite them to an event – a meeting, concert, activity or fundraiser of some kind. Neither is very complicated to organize, but there are a few things you should know.

News conferences

The standard news conference features somebody making an announcement, surrounded by reporters and cameras and with tape recorders on the table. This will almost never happen to you, unless you have something really big to say or someone very important is saying it. If you don't, refrain from holding a news conference; nothing creates a feeling of defeat like calling a news conference and having nobody show up. And nothing irks reporters more than making the effort to show up but finding a dull event.

That doesn't mean that what you have to say isn't important. It is just that with all the competing stories facing the news organization that day they have some hard decisions to make about what they will cover. A news conference may be the least appealing item for them, particularly for TV reporters: a shot of someone reading a prepared text does not make for interesting TV.

The other problem with news conferences is that they compel the media to adapt to your schedule. If reporters can't make it at the required time, they won't be able to report about your group. It is much better to tell the media that you have a major announcement to make and that a spokesperson from your organization is available all day to be interviewed. This gives the media maximum flexibility to respond to your news release and gives the interviewee a good one-on-one experience with each reporter.

If you still think you should call a news conference, here are a few simple guidelines to keep in mind.

- Hold it in a central location (e.g., downtown) so reporters can get to it easily.

- Alternatively, hold it in a place that illustrates what your group is doing – e.g., in front of an inner-city house that you are renovating, in a warehouse where relief supplies are being packaged, at a clinic where children are being treated.

- Think of the room setting. For example, don't place the podium against a large south-facing window (this is a bad angle for TV cameras). Find a pleasing background, such as a map of the world or photos of your group's activity.

- Set up the room so the speaker can sit at a table facing the reporters. Arrange the chairs so the TV cameras can be in the middle.

- Begin on time and end on time.

- Make sure reporters have a copy of the text of the announcement that will be shared at the conference. Some may have forgotten to bring along the information you sent out earlier.

- Have the spokesperson make a brief (5-minute) statement, with the remainder of the conference left for questions and answers.

- Make sure the speaker has enough time to do some one-on-one interviews after the formal part of the news conference is over.

- You may want to have coffee, tea and juice available as a courtesy, but this is not mandatory.

In general, news conferences should be reserved for major announcements involving large sums of money, wholesale changes in direction, glaring challenges to accepted public practice or government policy, or newsworthy events such as a famous personality joining your cause.

Media events

If you don't have a big announcement to make or a famous person to make it, how can you spread the word? One option is to hold an event that will be fun, meaningful and productive. Invite members of the media, but be sure that its success doesn't hinge on their attendance.

How can you do this? If your group is celebrating an anniversary or a special achievement, or is launching a new program or service, invite staff, volunteers, board members, clients and partners – along with the media – to join you for some cake and coffee. When the time is right, cut the cake, make a few statements, take some photos. If reporters come, great! If not, you still can have a fun time and make everyone feel good about your organization.

When you are inviting the media to an event, there are a few guidelines to follow.

- Greet the reporters when they arrive or as they circulate. Make sure they have a copy of the news release or other materials, and provide directions about how the event will unfold. This sounds obvious, but it is extremely important. Without a "quarterback" to direct the action, the experience can be frustrating for reporters, and perhaps for other staff, too, who may be annoyed to find a reporter taking up their time while they are trying to organize the event or keep a meeting going.

- Designate one or more persons to speak to the media at the event. Identify them in the news release you have sent out. Make sure everyone in your organization or on the event committee is comfortable with the choices. Other staff, board members and volunteers need to be "on message" – they need to stick to the topic and not distract reporters by talking about other programs or activities.

- Agree on what your spokespeople will say. What message are you trying to convey? You don't want any surprises, such as when I arranged for a pastor to speak about family violence at a church conference on that subject. He evidently got caught up in the moment because, during his remarks, he suddenly confessed that he, too, had once almost physically abused his daughter. His confession caught everyone by surprise, including me. You can guess what the headlines were the next day! If he had told me before the conference he was going to say this, I could have advised him of the consequences (i.e., he became the story, instead of the conference) and he could have calmly considered whether he wanted his admission splashed across newspapers and radio from coast to coast.

- Know that you aren't able to control what the story will be, as the above example shows. Reporters will report what they believe the story to be, not what you think it is. At a media event, many people can make comments to a reporter – from the president of the board, to the bishop of your church, to someone who thinks yours is the worst organization in the world and decided to stop by the event to let anyone who would listen (including a reporter) know. Be comfortable with this fact of life, or do not invite reporters to the event.

This advice holds true for meetings of any kind. Everyone at the meeting needs to know that everything is on the record. When you invite reporters to your denominational or organizational business sessions, they can report anything said from the platform or the floor, positive or negative. And since negative comments are often better copy than positive ones, an otherwise constructive three-hour meeting can sound as if it was filled with conflict when the reporter chooses to emphasize 10 minutes of heated and angry debate about an issue. As a reporter once said, "If I go to a meeting and a bomb goes off, I'm going to report about the explosion, not the meeting."

Of course, a public meeting is open to everyone, including reporters. The moment you put up posters, send out flyers or place an ad in a publication, you issue a blanket invitation to anyone who wants to come. Even when you choose not to invite reporters, they may ask to come (although they will not usually show up unannounced). Of course, they don't have time to attend every meeting in the hope that something interesting will occur, but be prepared in case they may be there.

- If you are bringing in a guest speaker from out of town for a week-end conference, arrange to have that person arrive the day before the event to be available for media interviews, especially if you need advance publicity to draw people to the event. If the speaker cannot come early, ask him or her to be available for telephone interviews before the event.

6

Other Media Opportunities

Here are some other ways to get media coverage besides sending a news release in the hope of securing an interview:

- op-ed submissions
- letters to the editor
- meeting with editors and news directors
- call-in shows
- public service announcements
- paid advertising
- free advertising
- special supplements
- rural media and suburban weeklies
- the alternative press
- sending reporters on trips to overseas projects.

Let's look at each one.

Op-ed submissions

Op-ed stands for "opposite the editorial page." This is the page where newspapers run opinion pieces submitted by readers, as well as regular columns and wire service commentary. An opinion article submitted to the op-ed page should be well written and succinct. (Most newspapers want something 700-800 words long.)

The op-ed page is prime real estate in the newspaper. For this reason, it is very difficult to get your submission placed there. Newspapers receive many submissions every day; a national newspaper such as *USA Today* gets around 150 credible unsolicited submissions a month, of which it may be able to publish 25 to 30, in the space not already committed to regular columnists.

What are the main factors in determining whether your submission will be published? The quality of the writing is probably the single most important consideration, and the first sentence is critical. Not only should it engage the editor immediately, it should convince him or her to keep reading. When an editor reads the piece, he or she will ask, "Will this piece grab the reader's attention? Once grabbed, will it hold their attention?"

The second factor is timeliness. Is the submission relevant to a current issue or debate? If something noteworthy happens on a Tuesday and you want to write something about it, write it Tuesday evening to improve your chances of it being accepted.

Another factor that can affect your chances of being published is authorship. Sometimes it is best to ask the executive director, board president, chief executive officer or bishop to write it (with your assistance), since this suggests that the opinion is an official statement.

Some electronic media also have op-ed–like features. In Canada, CBC radio has a commentary feature that airs across the country, while some radio and TV stations may provide listeners and viewers with "Your Turn" opportunities. You can request time in these slots by submitting a commentary piece to the media outlet. Remember that these need to be brief – no more than 2 minutes long (about two double-spaced pages).

Letters to the editor

One of the best-read sections of the newspaper is the letters to the editor. When you have a comment to make about an issue, but don't have enough time or material for an op-ed piece, the letters section is an excellent way to make a quick point. Even if your letter is not printed, it is read by an editor, which can influence coverage. Your comment might be used to spark another article.

As with anything else you send to the media, there is no guarantee that your letter will be published. Major daily newspapers receive many letters each day. *The Globe and Mail*, one of Canada's national newspapers, receives as many as 200 letters each day, of which it will print 12 to 18. When an issue attracts a lot of letters, the editor will pick a few representative letters.

Here are a few guidelines that can help your letter be considered for publication.

1. Respond as soon as possible to the article you are reacting to

The most common and best way today is by e-mail, which allows you to respond within hours of the newspaper landing on your doorstep. (You can also fax your letter just as quickly, but e-mail saves the newspaper the time and effort of retyping it.) Mail is fast becoming the least preferred way to send a letter. As Edward Greenspon, editor-in-chief of *The Globe and Mail*, notes, "By the time the few stragglers arrive by mail, the page has probably moved onto new issues."

2. Include your name, address and daytime phone number

Newspapers like to contact you to make sure you wrote the letter.

3. Include the title of the article and the date it was published

See #6 for an example of where to insert this information.

4. Stick to one issue

Don't write about several items.

5. Keep it short

Short letters (150 to 200 words) are more likely to be published than long ones.

6. Briefly restate the argument you wish to comment on, make your statement, then close

For example: "According to Joe Smith, religion is the bane of human-kind ("Religion a waste of time," Jan. 4.). He fails to take into consideration all the practical help offered by groups like the Salvation Army to society's down-and-outers – how many other groups do you see downtown handing out soup in freezing weather? People like the Salvationists believe that God calls them to serve others. Without them, our community would be a much poorer place."

7. Don't be abusive or offensive, and don't attack a particular person

Letters with that approach will not be printed.

8. Proofread

Check carefully for spelling and grammatical errors.

9. Avoid being part of letter-writing campaigns

Says Greenspon: "We are wary of organized letter-writing campaigns, which can easily be detected by the similarity of their wording. Such efforts can be counted on to squelch the enthusiasm of the letters editor."

Letters to the editor are read by many people. Take advantage of this vehicle to share your organization's point of view. The letters section is useful for adding information to a story, refuting an opinion in an article or praising the newspaper for carrying a story. Even when your letter is not printed, it is an excellent way to communicate your point of view to the newspaper.

Meeting with editors and news directors

Editors and news directors are approachable. You can arrange to meet with them to talk about concerns or to share information about your organization or the issue you are addressing. Such meetings should be set up with plenty of lead time, since editors and news directors have very busy schedules.

What should you talk about? Here in Winnipeg, a group of church communicators asked whether it could send some representatives to this city's largest daily paper to talk about religion coverage. They met with 10 reporters and editors, exchanging points of view about the coverage of religion by the paper. The communicators indicated that they wanted to learn more about how to help the newspaper tell religion stories; the editors and reporters shared tips about how to contact the paper, and what kinds of stories they were looking for.

Also in Winnipeg, I arranged for the president of an organization I worked for, and other senior staff, to meet the newspaper's editorial board to talk about a new approach to dealing with poverty in the developing world. Staff made a short presentation and the editors asked questions. The result was an editorial about this new approach a couple of days later, an invitation to submit an op-ed to the paper, and a request to let the editors know when the program was launched.

Meetings with members of the media don't have to be so formal. Take a reporter out to lunch or coffee (although he or she usually won't let you pay), or invite a reporter, editor or news director to speak to your staff or members at a meeting. These media figures are happy to talk to people in the community. These interactions can help to build understanding and relationships with the media.

Call-in shows

Call-in shows are both the most intriguing and most frightening opportunities available to you. They are intriguing because you can talk to average people; they are frightening because you have no idea how the show will go. Callers can be sympathetic, hostile, supportive and negative and everything in between, and so can the hosts!

Take advantage of call-in shows, but make sure that the person who is going to represent your organization is comfortable with the format. You can access call-in shows the same way you make yourself available to other media – with a news release indicating that someone is available to go on the show, or with a call to the show's producers. Since call-in shows tend to deal with current events, suggest ideas that centre on hot issues.

Call-in shows are often marked by their political leanings and the type of callers and listeners they attract. Some are more conservative, others more liberal. Make members of your organization available to the less sympathetic shows as well as the more sympathetic ones. It is important to share your organization's views with those who do not necessarily hold your opinions. Just make sure that whoever will appear on the show is willing to deal with critics, including the show's host.

Public service announcements

Almost all media outlets carry public service announcements (PSAs) of some sort. This could be a calendar of events in the newspaper, a radio show host reading a prepared script about an upcoming event, or a listing of events (with a voice-over) on a TV station.

PSAs are an important part of your media strategy. For radio, they are vital when the host has to fill 30 seconds or a minute of time between segments or before the news. The best way to send a PSA to a radio station is to prepare a short (25- to 35-second) script that the host can take straight off the pile and read – no need to do any shortening or editing. Make sure the "what, when, where and who" comes through loud and clear; in the short time available, you want to ensure people get the place, date and time. Here is an example.

Does the media do a better job of covering faith since 9/11? Or is it worse? Come hear *Winnipeg Free Press* editor Nicholas Hirst, Kirk LaPointe of CTV News, Gordon Legge of the Centre for Faith and Media, and Riad Saloojee of the Council on American-Islamic Relations address these questions and others on Monday, January 21, 7 p.m., Jubilee Place, 180 Riverton Ave. Admission is free.

Send out PSAs just as you do news releases – on your letterhead, with a request to the host to share it with listeners.

Some TV news shows also broadcast PSAs, either from the news desk or in a special voice-over segment. These may also run during the day in place of commercials.

If the same information were to be sent as an item for a community calendar in a newspaper, it could look like this:

January 21: Media coverage of faith since 9/11 with *Winnipeg Free Press* editor Nicholas Hirst, Kirk LaPointe of CTV News, Gordon Legge of the Centre for Faith and Media, and Riad Saloojee of the Council on American-Islamic Relations, 7 p.m., Jubilee Place, 180 Riverton Ave. Admission is free.

Again, the key is brevity. Check your local newspaper to see what style and format it uses.

Cable TV stations will also carry PSAs as printed text on a coloured background with music. There is a very specific letter count for these channels; contact your local cable provider for information and to see whether there is a form you can use to create your PSA.

There is no guarantee that a radio or TV station will use your PSA; they receive many requests. To help the editor decide which ones to use, he or she may employ a couple of yardsticks. For example, if the station is committed to causes such as literacy, a food bank or the heart fund, the editor will be disposed to using PSAs from groups that address those issues. He or she may also use the yardstick of money. Does your group advertise with the station? Sometimes the chances of getting your PSA on TV or radio improve when your group has a history of buying advertising on that station (or when your request for a PSA comes at the same time that you purchase advertising for the event).

Paid advertising

Speaking of advertising, you may believe that this avenue is closed to your group because it is too expensive, but most media outlets have special rates for non-profit groups or special deals (e.g., buy fifteen 30-second ads on a radio station, get five or ten additional ones free).

Be sure to ask media outlets what their non-profit rates are. When even that is too expensive, call a media outlet and tell them how much money you have, and ask how much advertising that will buy. It might not be enough, but even the few dollars you are offering are better than no dollars at all, so the media outlet may be willing to work out a deal with you if they have some space.

Free advertising

One way to get free advertising for an event is to enlist the media outlet as a sponsor. This usually involves the media outlet making an in-kind donation to the event in the form of a certain number of ads. The media outlet will require some kind of recognition from you in your event materials (e.g., poster and program) in return for the sponsorship. Most media outlets have a form they will send you to fill out and return when you ask them to be a sponsor; if you meet the requirements, they may agree to sponsor your event.

Another way to get free advertising for your group in newspapers is by creating camera-ready ads for them. These ads, which are made to exact specifications stipulated by the newspaper, perform the same service as PSAs do on radio: they fill holes. When laying out pages, composing room staff often have small spaces between articles, photos and ads that can be filled with the artwork you supply. Technically speaking, these are not ads, since there is no room for copy about events or services. But they will put your group's name and contact information in front of readers. Contact your local newspaper to see whether they do this; if they do, they will send you a list of the various sizes you can make ads for. Newspapers will keep these hole-fillers on file for a month or so, after which you need to resubmit them.

Special supplements

You have probably noticed that from time to time your local newspaper carries promotional material about home, garden, boat, craft or wedding shows. The pages are usually marked at the top with the word "advertisement" and feature ads from businesses related to the show in question. This is called an advertising supplement.

Non-profit groups can use supplements to promote events, such as an annual fundraiser or a walk-a-thon. Supplements can also be used to tell readers about a theme week (e.g., International Development Week in Canada) or commemorative days (e.g., International Women's Day, Earth Day). The supplements allow you to share important messages with readers, at no cost to you.

A supplement works like this. The newspaper divides the page between advertising and articles (the ratio is usually 50:50 or 60:40 ads to copy). You provide a list of potential advertisers to the newspaper (businesses that are owned by your supporters or that may be sympathetic to your cause). The sales department at the newspaper then contacts these businesses to see whether they will purchase an advertisement in the supplement. The number of pages of your supplement depends on the amount of advertising sold (e.g., if the newspaper sells half a page of ads, you get the other half for your event for articles and photos about your event). You can improve the chances that supporters who own businesses will take out ads by contacting them ahead of time and asking them to respond affirmatively when the sales representative from the newspaper calls. These ads typically feature the company's name and logo and something like "ABC Corporation says 'All the best!' to XYZ organization at its annual fundraiser!" The company can provide its own ad, or the newspaper can create it.

After securing the ads, the newspaper will assign a writer (usually a freelancer) to write a story about your group and the event. You will need to provide some people for the writer to interview, together with the usual background material. The newspaper may take some photos, or you can supply some that show your group in action. The supplement is usually slated to appear a day or two before your event, to maximize its impact.

After the supplement has been published, send a thank-you letter to the organizations that supported it. This helps pave the way for next year's supplement.

Rural media and suburban weeklies

Most non-profit organizations are located in large urban centres. Naturally, when they think of media coverage, they think of media outlets that are also located in, and serve, big cities. As a result, they miss good opportunities to share their messages with rural dwellers, via weekly newspapers (and, in some areas, rural radio stations).

For a couple of reasons, media outlets in smaller communities can be more open to material from your organization than are their urban counterparts. First, media outlets in smaller markets usually have small staffs; the editor may write stories, select articles, take photos and sell advertising. As a result, he or she will be receptive to well-prepared materials that can easily fill spaces (especially when the deadline for printing is looming and the editor has a hole or two to fill). If your news release is well written, timely and of interest to readers in that rural area, it might be published verbatim.

Keep the rural media in mind when you plan speaker tours. A visit by a group of Africans to talk about development can easily be overlooked in a big city, but it can be major news in small towns, which seldom get such visits. You may find it much easier to secure an interview with the local small-town paper or have a reporter come to your event in a smaller community than in a city.

Another opportunity for coverage is found in the suburban and neighborhood dailies and weeklies in cities. Yes, people often read them for the ads and coupons, but since these publications are local, they can help you reach a specific group of people in one part of your city. The weeklies are especially interested in events happening in their part of the city, or in people who come from those areas (e.g., a local person serving overseas).

The alternative press

The alternative press is made up of publications which are outside the mainstream media. This includes the thousands of activist newsletters with circulations of a few hundred, to larger periodicals such as *Mother Jones, Sojourners, This Magazine, The Progressive* and *The Utne Reader,* among others. Other vehicles include religious periodicals; peace and justice publications; newspapers that serve Aboriginal communities; and other magazines and newsletters that focus on subjects such as the environment, food and hunger, racism and many other issues. If your cause or issue intersects with their mandate, you can reach readers who are committed to a number of causes – people who could end up being your supporters and donors.

Sending reporters on trips to overseas projects

If you work for an international relief and development organization, you know that the best way for people to understand issues in the developing world is to see it for themselves. For this reason, consider inviting reporters to visit your projects overseas, or to join a tour. Don't be surprised if they say they can't, however. Few media outlets in North America today can afford to send reporters overseas, even when there is a strong local connection. You could offer to pay for the trip, but many media outlets will politely decline; they don't want anyone to think that you "bought" favourable coverage. In Canada, the Development Information Program of the Canadian International Development Agency (CIDA) pays up to 50 per cent of the cost of sending reporters overseas. Some media outlets participate, but others chafe at the requirement that they publicly acknowledge CIDA's support. You are most likely to be successful in getting smaller media outlets in rural communities to take you up on the offer. They rarely get a chance to travel overseas and may have fewer qualms about accepting a paid trip.

Sometimes it can be easier for a reporter to accept an invitation to travel overseas when more than one group issues the invitation, since media outlets do not want to be seen to be promoting one organization over others. This will dilute the focus on your group, but it may make it easier for the reporter to accept the invitation and lower your costs by spreading them around.

Another way to take reporters overseas is to ask them to be part of a tour composed of local people. This gives them a local angle and a group dynamic that they can be a part of. Still another option is a trip for several reporters from different, non-competing media outlets. Such a trip gives them a chance to feed off each other's impressions and ideas.

If a media outlet accepts your offer, here are a few things you should know.

• You don't have to pay for the whole trip. You could offer to take care of all in-country costs (food, lodging and transportation) if the media outlet pays for the flights.

• Provide some orientation, including details about the country, people and projects the reporter will visit and about your expectations for the trip. Local people will not distinguish between your organization and the reporter; if the reporter gets drunk in public or acts in a culturally inappropriate manner, local people will associate that negative behaviour with your group. For example, if you are going to a Muslim country, stress the fact that alcohol must not be consumed and explain other culturally inappropriate ways of acting (e.g., in some countries men should never strike up a conversation with a woman they don't know or be alone in a house with a woman they aren't married to). You will also need to give the reporter information about immunizations (when needed) and encourage him or her to check into health and other insurance coverage. You may also need to get him or her to sign a waiver to release your organization from liability in the event of an accident or illness (check with a lawyer about this issue).

• Be prepared to give the reporter the freedom to follow his or her own leads. The stories will be much more credible when they are not merely puff pieces, but rather serious reports about important issues. The ground rules going into the trip must be that you will not place any limits on what the reporter will report about, and you will not ask to preview the report before it is published or broadcast. If this is too risky, don't invite a reporter to go overseas with you.

- After the trip ends, ask the reporter to share his or his experience with your supporters. You cannot require a reporter to do anything more than file a report about the trip, but most are glad to meet with your supporters to talk first-hand about the visit and answer questions.

7

Religion and the Media

Introduction

One thing people from different faith groups agree on is this: the media does a poor job of covering religion.

A 2003 Canadian survey found that 63 per cent of people who regularly go to worship services believe the media misses the mark when it comes to reporting about religion.

When the media does report about religion, people of faith complain that reporters seem to know little about the subject. Some reporters can't tell a priest from a pastor and don't know whether a Corinthian is someone featured in a book of the Bible or a style of column. When it comes to non-Western religions, the problem is magnified.

Why is coverage so poor? Part of the problem lies with the media, of course. Reporters often fail to see religion as a subject worth covering, or are uncomfortable talking about spirituality and faith. The absence of a religion beat at many North American media outlets means there is nobody available who understands the intricacies and nuances of religious groups and beliefs.

Reporters could certainly do a better job of reporting about religion, but the fault is not all theirs. Faith groups could also do a much better job of communicating with the media. But many religious groups are wary of dealing with the media because they believe reporters to be anti-religious. This conviction is bolstered every time there are negative reports about their faith group. They are afraid that reporters have a hidden agenda to search for scandal or impropriety.

While it is true that some people who work in the media are unsympathetic to religion, it is not true that most members of the media are anti-religious. What they are is pro good stories. A news director at an Ontario radio station was proud to say that he was an atheist. But something he was even prouder of was that his station presented its listeners with good stories. If a reporter could convince him that a story was good, it didn't matter whether it was about God or faith; he would run it. Making sure you send the media good stories is key to getting coverage.

That said, it is true for some in the media that religion is simply irrelevant. It is irrelevant personally, because they have no personal faith convictions and, thus, aren't aware of the importance of religion to many people. As a result, says Richard Handler, executive director of CBC Radio's *Tapestry* program, those who appreciate the sacred have a problem trying "to get the attention of those who don't know what the sacred is, and are suspicious of religion anyway."

He goes on to say, "The mainstream media is full of secular types. They pride themselves in their skeptical view of the world, whether true or not. They know enough about history to know that religion has been used to justify the worst sorts of atrocities, and religious faith isn't open to the usual rules of evidence. Also, in our culture religion has become a private affair. So how religious people or institutions approach matters of public policy can be a source of great confusion."

Religion is also irrelevant to many in the media in a broader sense. They see religion as something that happens behind the closed doors of places of worship. They don't believe that religion and religious groups have anything relevant to say about the issues that concern the majority of people. By working with the media, faith groups can help reporters see that religion has a great deal to say about the issues that face society, and that many people are putting their faith into action by addressing racism, violence, poverty, sexual abuse, hunger, the environment and other issues.

Sharing religion stories with the media

If you are going to share stories about your group with the media, here are a few things you should know.

1. Reporters are not interested in your services and meetings

A former reporter, recalling his days at a radio station, says that while he regularly received communications from churches, synagogues and temples "inviting me to talk about rummage sales and those sorts of fundraising events, I didn't very often get things from churches or synagogues or temples talking about issues or things in the news."

Gathering together for worship and prayer – and rummage sales and other fundraising events – is important to the life of faith communities. But these happenings are seldom of interest to the media. One reason is that reporters are interested in things that are new and different. Activities that happen every week on the same day and at the same time are not new or different. As an editor of a large city daily newspaper pointed out, the mere fact that many thousands of people go to church each Sunday doesn't make it a story. "Lots of people use the bus each day and that doesn't make that a story either," he said.

Similarly, reporters are usually not interested in your conferences and other meetings. These events may be crucial to the life of your group, but they are very difficult to report about since they are often mainly about in-house matters. Plus, these meetings often take place over the span of several days or more. A media outlet can rarely dedicate that much of a reporter's time to cover the entire event.

If you do want to invite the media to cover a meeting, identify something that reporters might be interested in covering – something that has implications for the wider community (e.g., discussion about a new anti-poverty program) or that has a substantial effect on your group (e.g., a new policy that changes a traditional understanding of scripture or a traditional practice, such as not ordaining women). Reporters may also be interested in people who are speaking at or attending meetings (e.g., someone with a fascinating conversion story, someone involved in a ministry that addresses societal issues, someone who is an outspoken critic of a government policy or a societal trend such as government-sponsored gambling).

2. Media outlets do not promote religious points of view

When it comes to religious belief, the media is not in the business of trying to determine which group has the truth. The role of the media is to present various points of view and let people make up their own minds. By not suggesting that your group is right, media outlets are not against you; if they did promote one faith group over others, they would be open to charges of being unbalanced or unfair. Since the media serves a multicultural and multi-religious audience, reporters are keen to avoid giving offence to any group. For this reason, reporters are also often reluctant to cover one group's efforts to evangelize.

3. Reporters need religious people to help them understand how groups are organized

Reporters need someone to guide them through the maze of denominational and other faith groups. Baptists, for example, may know the difference between Regular, Federation, General or Free Will Baptists (to name a few), but how is a reporter supposed to know? The same is true for other groups. What do the various branches of Islam believe? How are they different? Are all Hindus the same? What are the differences between the 25 Mennonite denominations? For a reporter unfamiliar with the various groups, it can be extremely difficult to sort out who belongs where or which group gets the credit (or blame) for what. Someone is needed to help a reporter through this maze. Creating a media guide to your group can be a good first step.

4. Knowledge about religion can no longer be assumed

It is becoming cliché to say that we live in a post-religious age. In North America, which has long considered itself to be based on Judeo-Christian values, the beliefs and biblical knowledge that Jews and Christians take for granted are unknown to many people, including many who work in the media. (For example, one US poll found that most Americans have no idea what terms such as "the Great Commission," "John 3:16" and "the Gospel" mean.) When it comes to non-Western religions, knowledge is even scantier. In other words, theological understandings and scriptural images that are commonplace for you and your group can be completely foreign to reporters. If you want to work with the media, be careful about the language you use and be sure to explain what various concepts, allusions and events mean.

5. The religion page

For some people, the religion page is a sign of how seriously a newspaper takes religion; for others, it is a religious ghetto where a few stories are printed to keep all the church advertisers happy. Whatever your opinion, the religion page is a staple of most daily newspapers in North America. It deserves your support.

At some newspapers, the religion reporter is an integral part of the operation and the beat is highly respected. Typically, these are newspapers that do not confine religion coverage to the Saturday religion page, but rather ones at which reporters are encouraged to try to write stories that can appear throughout the newspaper during the week. At these papers, religion stories are not viewed as filler, but reflect the paper's view that religion is an important part of the life of the community. If you live in a community that is served by such a newspaper, voice your approval regularly through letters or phone calls.

At other newspapers, the religion beat is viewed as the worst job a reporter could have, only slightly better than writing obituaries. When one major Canadian paper wanted to reduce staff, it assigned a reporter it wanted to lay off to the religion beat in the hope she would be so dissatisfied with the assignment that she would quit. She decided to get her revenge by doing the best job she could. She kept her job and, to her surprise, also discovered that she liked the beat!

Newspapers that have good religion pages are to be commended. The editors and reporters need to be encouraged to see religion as a subject that should appear in other sections, too. As good as a religion page may be, the only people who read it are religious people. Other readers don't get to see the active role that religion plays in the lives of other members of the community.

Whatever kind of religion coverage you have, voice your support for it. In these days of cost-cutting, the religion beat is increasingly under scrutiny. When the city editor is down to three reporters, he or she may well wonder how on earth the paper can afford to keep one reporter full-time on religion. Regular support for the beat by readers can make the difference between keeping it or letting it go.

One thing that is important to remember is that religion reporters don't operate according to a schedule. ("Let's see. I did Baptists two weeks ago, Muslims last week. It's time for the Pentecostals.") They operate according to the same principles as those of every other beat at the paper. Is there any news? Your chances of being covered increase when you let the reporter know what your church or organization is doing.

6. The "secular" media

Many religious people describe the media as "the secular media." Technically speaking, the mainstream media is secular, as opposed to being sacred – that is, it is not a religious press. But the word "secular" carries pejorative connotations for many religious people today. It is almost shorthand for something definitely bad, if not downright evil. But news organizations are not evil or bad. Rather than calling the media "secular," just call it "the media" or "the non-religious media." After all, a lot of religious people work for the media, and they view their work as a God-given calling.

7. Religious people in the media

Many people of faith work for the media. They bring their faith to work with them. But like their non-religious colleagues, they have to obey the rules of their workplace. They have to be fair and objective. They have to report both sides of a story, even when they don't agree with one side. This can cause problems for them with their faith group. If it opposes gambling, but they have to write a story about a casino, they can be seen as contradicting the beliefs of their group. If something like this happens to a reporter from your group, avoid making a judgment: the reporter was only doing his or her job. Likewise, don't think that because a reporter is religious he or she is "on your side." Reporters will try to represent your point of view fairly, but they will have to report the opposite viewpoint fairly, too.

As well, don't expect a reporter who is religious to go out of his or her way to report about every religiously oriented story possible. While the reporter may be more sensitive to those kinds of stories, and may even lobby occasionally to make sure some are reported, he or she has to be careful not to be seen as an advocate for one group or another. In some cases, reporters who belong to a particular faith group try to avoid reporting about those groups, in order to prevent any suggestions of conflict of interest or favouritism (and to avoid being criticized by faith group members if the story is negative).

8. Work with other faith groups to promote religion

Since the media is wary of being seen to be promoting one religion over others, a good way to encourage reporters to pay more attention to the subject is by presenting a united front with other faith groups on this issue. You can do this by sending representatives from various groups to a meeting with the media. Call the editor or news director and say you'd like learn more about how faith groups can assist the media when it comes to covering religion, and to tell them about the religious community in your city. In Winnipeg, where I live, such a meeting resulted in greater understanding on both sides, and a request from the city's largest daily newspaper for a list of faith groups and contact names.

9. Why religious groups should have a media plan

It used to be that crises were handled within the faith community. There was a collective understanding that problems were dealt with quietly within the walls of the church, synagogue, mosque or temple. Rarely, if ever, were outsiders such as the courts and the media called upon.

Things are different today. While many problems are still handled within the community, some people seek redress outside the group. When an issue becomes public, the media can become involved. This is particularly true in the case of abuse.

Any faith group that is actively involved in serving the community, especially children, needs a media plan. While parents who are members of the group may take their concerns and allegations to the membership, some who do not belong to the group may go to the media first. The time to learn how to work with the media over an allegation of abuse is not when a reporter calls to inquire about the situation.

Religious groups need a crisis plan, just as other non-profit organizations do. (For information on creating a crisis communications strategy, see Chapter 8.)

Thoughts from journalists about covering religion

The 1998 Faith and the Media conference in Ottawa featured sessions in which journalists answered this question: What do reporters wish faith groups knew about how the media works? Here are a few comments from that session. (Note: The job titles are the ones the panelists held in 1998.)

Royal Orr, former radio reporter and host of CBC's
Cross Country Check-Up

Talk about issues

"I regularly received things from churches, synagogues and temples inviting me to talk about rummage sales and those sorts of fundraising events. I didn't very often get things from churches or synagogues or temples talking about issues or things in the news. Even though I knew that the national organizations that these churches and synagogues were part of were talking about important issues, I found it odd that the materials that the national churches were preparing weren't interesting enough for local churches to send them along to me, but that's something the churches have to deal with, I guess."

Good stories are important

"When making up my mind about what to discuss, one of the things I had to confront each morning was that our director of news and public affairs was proudly atheistic. But like any good reporter or good editor, the thing he was even prouder about was that his radio station presented its listeners with good stories and he always wanted to hear about good stories. And if at a story meeting you could convince him that it was a good story or the grist for a good discussion, whether it was about religion or faith or something else, he didn't mind."

Get to know the media

"What ends up being covered is very much a function of the individuals who come up with the ideas in those story meetings. And if there is a journalist or some journalists or an editor or some editors who seem to be interested in matters of faith and religion, you should cultivate those people. You should suggest ideas to them. You should support them as they fight for story ideas. And when they actually get something to air or into print, you should reward them by making sure that their bosses know that you appreciated that kind of reporting and that kind of issue being dealt with, even if you don't agree with the specific take that a reporter has on a story."

You might not like the result

"If you're going to play the media game and work to get yourself covered, you're not going to always like the way the media treats your story or your organization. I'm afraid that's part of the game as well."

Peter Cavanagh,
producer on CBC Radio's This Morning

Agendas are different

"One thing that faith groups should know about the CBC is that their agendas are different from ours. They have a particular issue that they're obsessed with and we may well, and often do, see the issue differently. Faith groups are often convinced of the goodness or rightness of their cause and often don't see the necessity or fairness of an opposing view. Faith is often a question of pure belief. Journalism is often an exercise in skepticism. These two views of the world can clash."

Educating journalists

"The person a faith group approaches may be unfamiliar with the faith in question, and the members of the faith group may need to be tolerant of the journalist's lack of knowledge. Just as an expert in a particular field might have to educate the journalist, so too the faith group member might need to educate. A journalist's lack of knowledge about a particular faith is not a slight, but simply a reality."

Different views on timing and ways to tell stories

"A national media operation has time and budget constraints and pro-gramming needs that are not always understood by people outside. Faith groups sometimes have to accept that their timing and ours will not coincide. As well, we have a particular view of what constitutes a good story and what elements are necessary in the telling of a good story. Faith groups might find this difficult to accept, but getting angry about the way we want to tell a story won't make the dialogue easier."

How to make it easier for the media

"First, accept that we won't always see eye to eye. Second, be clear about what the story is and how it is of interest to people outside the faith group. Third, be open when we want to talk about a story and not just when they want to talk about a story. Fourth, don't assume from the word go that we are biased and/or unwilling to learn. Don't assume that because we disagree, we are prejudiced."

Alex Frame, director of programming, CBC English radio

Faith in the newsroom

"As far as CBC Radio is concerned, we are not made up of agnostic or atheist secular liberal thinkers. There is a significant number of people, including me, who take religion and their own religion very seriously. So it is not for lack of fundamental sympathy with spiritual issues that these difficulties arise. I would suggest it is a mistake on the part of any of us to assume that in dealing with people within the media you're dealing with a group of people who have turned their backs on spirituality or religion. It just isn't the case. But that doesn't mean that they're particularly fixed on a particular religious view."

Expand the debate

"If there's one thing that faith groups could do to expand the nature of public discourse, understanding, enlightenment and wisdom, it is to expand the debate. The debate needs expansion. By that, I mean adding one's voice to other voices that are commenting on the issues of the day, or adding one's voice to the voices that are already saying that we need to have the social structure turned over to have more sympathy and support for the poor. The debate, however, will not be expanded by absolutist doctrinaire statements. That closes down the debate."

Casey Korstanje, religion reporter, Hamilton Spectator

Not searching for scandal

"Let me give you some tips about how to deal with the media. We're not always searching for the sensational to make you look bad or to focus on those things. Those things happen and we will write about them, but what is not good for you folks out there is if your first contact with the media or with a journalist is because you're now in a damage-control mode over something. If that's the first time you've talked to a reporter, you're not going to get the kind of sympathetic coverage you want."

Pauline Finch-Durichen, religion reporter,
Kitchener-Waterloo Record

Deadlines are real

"I wish people who contact me knew that production deadlines are real. I can't do end runs around deadlines to get that last strawberry social in even if it is to raise money to put roofs over people's heads, to really help people. I wish people wouldn't call me so late. When groups are planning an event they will have a list of 23 things to do to prepare for this event; number 22 will be to call the *Record*. 'Oh, yes, but it happens tomorrow.' 'Okay, I'm afraid I can't do anything. I can report on it after it has happened. How much money did you raise doing this? This is great, but if you'd told us a little sooner we might find a story inside that story that will surprise us, that will surprise you.' "

Every contact is important

"We may not have a story out of every contact. If you can live with the fact that not every contact with me or any other reporter will result in a story, but will result in connections, then perhaps you'll see, farther on down the line, that you do build up that critical mass of interest, of passion, of engagement. All of a sudden I'll run across an issue and say, 'I remember I talked to Jane Doe about six months ago; I wonder if she's still the media liaison for that group. I wonder if she's still working for that church. I'll call her. She's probably got something to say about that.' "

Reporters don't have the final say on a story

"I don't have unlimited power to determine what a story looks like in the paper or how the photo caption or the headlines are going to look. I can have some limited input in how a story is edited in terms of what's taken out or left in, but mainly once I've done a story I have to trust, again, higher powers, as well. Sometimes it calls for understanding and sometimes it calls for me calling up and saying, 'Well, it didn't turn out quite the way we had hoped, but my editor saw something else, another issue that I hadn't anticipated. My editor is keeping many, many balls in the air.' "

Conclusion

Helping journalists find their way through the faith group maze is an important goal, but helping faith groups make it easier for reporters to get information is equally vital. Poor faith coverage isn't always the media's fault; many faith groups are poorly prepared to deal with the media. They don't know how the media works, how to contact reporters or how to write a news release. When reporters do call, faith groups often don't have spokespersons who are comfortable doing interviews.

Sometimes, despite all the problems, good coverage results. But other times it is incomplete or inaccurate, which only feeds the suspicion held by many people of faith that the media is anti-religious. That is seldom, if ever, the case; in more than two decades of working in media relations for various faith-related groups, I have met only one editor who claimed to be anti-religious. Poor faith coverage is more likely to occur because an ill-trained reporter has had to deal with a faith group that is ill-prepared for working with the media.

A number of good sources of information about religion and the media exist in North America. Here are several you will want to check out.

• The Centre for Faith and the Media offers information and assist-ance for working with the media in Canada. According to Director Richelle Wiseman, the centre exists to help the media report about religion because "the number of stories about faith and spirituality is increasing, but journalists are not always well-prepared to cover them. We can help provide background, context and contacts for them." The Centre has produced guides for journalists on Christian-ity, Islam and Judaism, and plans to provide workshops for report-ers on covering religion. It also offers media relations workshops.

You can contact the Centre by calling 1-877-210-0077, or visit the website at www.faithandmedia.org.

- The US-based Leonard E. Greenberg Center for the Study of Religion in Public Life publishes *Religion in the News*, a thrice-yearly magazine that covers media reporting of religion as part of the Program on Religion and the News Media. For more information, go to www.trincoll.edu/depts/csrpl/default.htm. The site contains a list of links to other sources of information on the topic of faith and media.

- The Religion Newswriters Association (www.rna.org) is a non-profit association of more than 200 mostly US-based religion reporters. Founded in 1949 to advance the professional standards of religion reporting in the press, as well as to create a support network for religion reporters, the association strives to help improve and encourage religion writing excellence in the press.

8

Crisis Communications

A lmost every organization will experience a crisis that involves the media at some point. Neighbours could oppose a group's building plans. A shipment of food sent overseas could go astray or be spoiled in transit. A staff person could be accused of sexual misconduct. The treasurer might be caught stealing donations. A child from the community could be seriously injured at a day camp. What do you do when you have phone messages from five reporters?

If that is the first question on your mind when a crisis hits, you have already broken the number-one rule of crisis communications: *Prepare for a crisis before it happens.* You do this by creating a crisis communications strategy.

Crisis communications strategy

A crisis communications strategy is not a complicated thing. It simply sets out how to decide when you have a crisis that needs public acknowledgment, who will respond to the media when a crisis hits, how he or she will respond, and who needs to be involved in decisions about the release of information. A crisis plan should accomplish the following things:

Help you decide on the nature of the crisis

Some crises will never come to the media's attention. Some may be brought to your attention by the media. Before issuing a news release, ask, Do reporters know about the crisis already? Are they likely to know? How widely do you need to share the information? Once you have answers to these questions, you will know how much energy you need to expend communicating about the crisis, and whom you need to communicate with. Just remember: there are no secrets. Even if you think reporters will not find out (e.g., it is an internal crisis), prepare as if they will. A general rule for whether you need to inform the media is this: the greater the public profile of the person or program in question, the more public the disclosure needs to be.

Choose the spokesperson(s)

When something needs to be said publicly about the crisis, select someone to speak to the media and to others. It could be the executive director or someone appointed by the executive director. You want only one person to speak to the media. The greater the number of people who are speaking during a crisis, the greater the likelihood that they will make widely varying remarks. You could appoint one person to speak to the media and another to deal with internal communications to staff, the board, volunteers, donors and clients.

List everyone in the organization who is to be informed about the crisis

Staff and board members should not learn about the crisis from the media or from other avenues outside the organization. Inform them early in the crisis through meetings or other internal communication channels, and keep them informed as things develop or change. When the crisis involves a volunteer or staff member serving in an overseas location, appoint someone to communicate directly with that person's family, to be their conduit of information.

Indicate how communications will be prepared and approved during a crisis

How will decisions be made about what to say to the media? Who will write the news releases? Who will approve them – the board? senior staff? Create a committee composed of a senior staff person, a member of the board, someone from the media or communications department, and other staff. The key is not to make the chain too long; you will need to be able to respond quickly when a crisis occurs. You won't have the luxury of waiting a few days until the board chair is back from a business trip to approve a news release so you can send it out.

Dealing with a crisis

Issue a news release

When you have a crisis that reporters already know about, or will be interested in, the first thing to do is to issue a news release containing a statement from your organization. This statement should acknowledge the crisis (trying to pretend it doesn't exist is a poor strategy) and explain your understanding of the nature of the crisis (as much as you know at that point) and what you are doing about it. It is important to demonstrate some kind of action, even when that action is meeting to talk about what kind of action to take.

Do not announce a solution too quickly

For example, when the crisis involves abuse, information may come from the offender slowly (e.g., admitting to a one-time incident, then later to multiple incidents with one victim, and possibly later acknowledging that there were many victims). Always couch your responses with the phrase "As far as we know now." This gives you room to manoeuvre if the situation changes. You never want to be publicly forced to backtrack or admit you were wrong or hasty in judgment. This creates a lack of confidence and instills doubt in future pronouncements. Additionally, when your chief source of information is the offender or friends and family of the offender, say so. ("What we have been told by the offender is…." "According to people close to the offender….") Otherwise, the credibility of your statements will be called into question.

When the crisis is ongoing, release a statement whenever there is a significant development to keep the media (and others) informed.

Never downplay or make jokes about a crisis

In the 1990s, an animal rights group claimed to have sabotaged some Canadian ice cream bars because it believed animals were injured in product testing. The owner of the company that made the bar learned of the crisis only when a reporter called. The owner thought the animal rights group was accusing him of using animal parts in his bars. Said he, "As far as I know, we don't grind up any mice to make our bar." That quote became front-page news across Canada and the owner spent days trying to retract it. He learned a valuable lesson from the experience: don't make wisecracks about a crisis. You don't want to read your "joke" on the front page tomorrow. Remember that when a reporter calls, everything is on the record, including your attempts at humour.

Never assume that you can keep a crisis or problem a secret

There is very little in the world that the media doesn't know about or can't find out about. People in the media know people in your organization, or know someone who does (e.g., a staff member's brother is dating a girl whose brother is best friends with a reporter at the local newspaper).

See whether there is a way to turn a problem to your advantage

In the 1980s, a relief group I worked with sent a food shipment to a wartorn country in Africa. Soon after it arrived, the aid began to go astray – actually, people started stealing the food the moment it left the boat. We realized we had a crisis. Ordinary Canadians had given us hundreds of thousands of dollars to buy that food and send it to starving people. We issued a news release about the missing food and used the unfortunate situation as a "teachable moment," an opportunity to let the media and the public know just how hard it is to do relief work during a war. The loss of the food provided an opportunity to talk about how one of the best solutions to hunger is peace and security. This forthright approach helped us to preserve our reputation as a trustworthy aid organization and, at the same time, taught people about the relationship between war and hunger.

Tell the truth

Sometimes the truth can be painful, particularly when it involves the fall of someone in a position of moral authority. For religious groups, this can be particularly difficult. But as one reporter has said about Christianity, if the church can't tell the truth about itself, whom can you trust it to tell the truth about? By telling the truth you can help reporters understand that members of your group are not immune from wrong behaviour. This non-defensive approach can help build bridges of understanding to the media and the community during a very painful time.

If your organization is at fault, take full responsibility

In other words, don't pass the buck. Don't blame others. Admit you were wrong. Acknowledge that the oversight was regrettable. You will not gain public trust by shirking responsibility. Say you were at fault, but then go on to say what you are doing to make sure the same thing never happens again. (Before you speak, you may want to check with a lawyer to ascertain the legal implications of your forthright admission.)

Don't let reports about the crisis be the final word about your organization. After the crisis is over, send information to your supporters or to the media within a couple of weeks. Talk about other things that are happening in the organization. Report about the positive results of your work. You don't want to let the bad news be the only thing that people remember.

Sharing bad news

When something bad happens to your organization, there are two ways to deal with it. One is to hope that nobody notices and that the problem will go away. Unfortunately, this usually doesn't work; there is very little that is secret in the world today. The second way is to initiate the coverage yourself. Come clean, admit the problem, spill the details.

When a reporter initiates contact about a problem, you are immediately on the defensive. Among other things, a reporter will want to know how long you have known about the problem. If it has been a while, he or she will want to know why you have not informed the public. Is it a cover-up? As we all know, cover-ups are among the greatest sins in the eyes of the media.

Even when the reporters don't find out, news about the problem is sure to leak out in other ways. It is like the old children's game of broken telephone: someone tells someone, who tells someone else, who in turn tells another. By the time the news gets to the end of the chain, it is wildly inflated and sensationalized.

By sharing bad news in an open and forthright manner, you get to go on the offensive. You can set the margins and terms of the discussion, provide the angles and shape the story. People (including reporters) will respond to the news you share, not the other way around. At the same time, sharing bad news shows that you are treating the matter seriously.

But sharing bad news doesn't always mean sending a news release to the media. You can use other communication channels just as effectively. For example, when $400,000 was stolen by local staff in Africa from an organization I worked for, we wrote about the fraud in our own publication, which was sent to more than 5,000 people across North America. We also put it on our website. At the same time, we informed the religious press, and they carried reports about the situation. Later, when a reporter from a national newspaper called to ask about the stolen money, I could say, "Sure, I'd be happy to talk about it. And could I send you copies of the articles that have been published about it?"

He published a short story, but the wind was taken out of his sails. There was no cover-up, no attempt to keep it quiet, no deepening scandal. In other words, there was no scoop. We had already spilled the beans on ourselves. You can do the same with your own publication and website, and through other periodicals.

If some people in your organization resist this strategy, remind them that hoping the problem will go away may only end up dragging it out. In the end, it won't hurt any less; it will only hurt longer.

If reporters show up at your door one day to cover something such as abuse or misconduct, don't be angry. Instead, be grateful. Think of how much worse it would be if the media didn't take note at all. This would mean that reporters see misconduct as normal, or not unusual, behaviour for leaders of non-profit organizations and religious groups! The fact that reporters take note of these failings indicates that society still holds high standards for people who occupy leadership positions in these kinds of groups. And we can be grateful for that.

9

Miscellaneous

What to do when the media gets it wrong

Mistakes are a part of life. The difference with errors in media coverage is that the mistakes are out in the open for all to see. (As an old adage says, "Doctors bury their mistakes. Editors publish theirs.") What should you do when there is a mistake in a report about your organization?

First, make sure you have a legitimate complaint. Is it a major error on which the main point of the report hinges, or a misspelled name? Is it something that is likely to change the impact of the report or the impression of your organization in the mind of readers? If not, don't worry about it. The average reader probably hasn't noticed.

When you do have a legitimate complaint, don't rant and rave at the reporter, editor or news director. As a reporter once said, "We've been threatened by the best, and it fails to move us." Also avoid making sweeping generalizations about coverage ("You only report negative stories about Baptists!"). News outlets have published plenty of stories about Baptists over the years, including many positive ones, and reporters and editors can itemize each one for you.

When a newspaper prints an error that you feel should be corrected, bring it to the attention of the editor. He or she may print a clarification or correction. You could also write a letter to the editor to correct the error. A conversation with an editor might also result in a request to write an op-ed piece in which you can clarify your organization's point of view.

Broadcast media will also correct errors, although they don't have "our mistake" sections like newspapers do. Again, call or write the news director or host to tell them about the error.

When you feel that a newspaper headline was misleading or sensationalized, do not complain to the reporter. Reporters do not write their own headlines. This is a specialized task in the newsroom. Talk to the editor about it.

Remember: what seems to be a major problem to you may not be major to many others. Try to keep this in perspective. A bad reputation is never the result of one story (and neither is a good one). Perceptions about whether an organization is good or bad are built up over time. Organizations usually do not fall on the basis of one erroneous statement.

When an interview doesn't result in an article or report

Sometimes it is not that the reporter got it wrong, but that the news outlet didn't report anything at all. You may have spent 20 minutes on the phone with a reporter. Maybe a TV crew came out to your news conference. The next day you searched the newspaper for the article; you turned page after page, but it wasn't there. Or you watched the news, but the report didn't appear. What happened?

One of the expectations we bring to an interview is that the results of it will be printed or broadcast. This isn't unreasonable. Why would a media outlet go to all the trouble of sending out a reporter if it didn't intend to publish or broadcast something?

One reason an article or report can fail to appear is that something more important bumped it from the news lineup. In the 1980s, I helped two Sudanese visiting Canada to obtain an interview with a national Canadian news show. They were ecstatic about the chance to tell Canadians about the then-untold story about the terrible civil war in their country. The news network conducted an in-depth interview in the morning; later that day a commercial airliner crashed in Canada. Suddenly everything else the network had prepared to put on the news that day was pushed aside by the breaking story of the crash. The interview about Sudan never appeared. Naturally, the Sudanese visitors were extremely disappointed.

Another reason an interview can fail to appear is that the reporter "wrote it out of the newspaper." The story is basically fine, but the reporter was unable to write it in an interesting way or didn't support the article with enough facts or quotes. As a result, the editors might "kill" it, rather than let something that failed to meet their standards be printed or aired. It can sometimes appear later, after the reporter has added the missing material or another reporter has had a chance to polish it.

Sometimes a report fails to appear because the reporter never intended to publish anything at all. In other words, the reporter was fishing – talking to you to see whether there was a story. After talking to you, the reporter might decide there is no story. As a result, the idea gets dropped and nothing appears.

These experiences can be disappointing and frustrating. After all, you spent considerable time and effort answering the reporter's questions. It is not inappropriate to call the editor or news director and ask what happened to the story. It is possible that a conversation with you might convince the editor or news director that the story has merit after all, and he or she might assign another reporter to complete it.

Should you ask reporters to join your board?

No. Why? Because it compromises their ability to be good reporters. A reporter I know loves the theatre. But when theatre groups ask him to join their boards, he always declines. If he did join the board of a theatre company, he could not report about that company as long as he held the position. It would be a conflict of interest. Plus, he might have to stop reporting about theatre altogether, for fear that a negative review might cause someone to think he did it because he supports a rival group.

This doesn't mean that reporters won't actively support your group. They may participate in events to raise money for health research because they have an illness or know someone who does. They might be members of your organization. But they will generally resist efforts to be publicly identified with your group (e.g., to be seen to be endorsing it) for fear that this will compromise their ability to be fair.

"Famine pornography"

Organizations that assist people who have needs – hungry people in the developing world, poor people, minorities, Aboriginal people, people with disabilities and people living with HIV/AIDS, among others – need to be careful about the language they use to describe them. In your communication efforts, avoid using language and images that are insensitive. If you aren't careful, you could end up creating "famine pornography."

Famine pornography is any image or report that objectifies an individual or group of people. The term was coined to describe how the media (and some relief groups) show or describe people in the developing world – just showing the negative, or the worst, about a group or country.

It is true that many negative things occur in some developing countries. But there is more than just famine, disaster, hunger, disease, war and poverty. What about friendship? Faith? Family? Work? Sports? These, too, are part of life in those countries, although you might be hard-pressed to find out about them in much of the media.

It is easy to blame the media for this situation. Since media outlets want to report news, and since a famine is news, it seems that this is all they report about in a developing country. Reporters certainly could do a better job of reporting the whole scope of life in the developing world, but relief and development groups must also share some of the blame. Surveys in Canada have shown that, when it comes to negative attitudes towards the developing world, relief and development groups have contributed to the problem through their fundraising materials. A 1990 Canadian study noted, "Much of their past communication efforts have focused on the horrible situations in some of the poorer countries of the world. They have constantly reminded people of how serious the situation is. This is an important step in creating awareness. However, after years of exposure to these heart-wrenching messages, and no apparent success in alleviating any of these problems, people lose hope, and then interest."

These findings were supported by a 1991 study sponsored by the Canadian Council for International Co-operation, an umbrella group for Canadian relief and development agencies. The study said the use of heart-wrenching images from the developing world might bring in lots of money, but in the long term it produces a sense of despair that nothing can be done to help people in poorer countries. The study also suggested that years of exposure to images of famines, disasters and starving children can cause the opposite of what relief groups intend. Instead of becoming informed, enthusiastic supporters of overseas development, Canadians may question whether there is any point in giving money to support relief and development work overseas.

At the same time, the use of negative images creates the false impression that people in the world's poorer countries are pathetic victims incapable of helping themselves. They are seen to be passive bystanders, completely dependent on outside help. A steady diet of this material can lead to the dangerous notion of North American superiority, as well as a deep-seated paternalism.

What is true for international development assistance is true for other issues as well. But how can you make sure that your communications avoid sending unintentional negative messages?

Watch your language

How do you talk about the people you are trying to assist? Using short-hand expressions such as "the hungry," "the disabled" or "the poor" risks objectifying human beings. They are "hungry people," "people with disabilities" or "poor people." This reminds us all that we are talking about people, not economic or physical categories. Also, think about the words you use to describe what you do. Do you only "help" others? Or do you "work with" them, too? How you describe your efforts can go a long way towards affirming the strength and dignity of others, or it can cast them as helpless victims dependent on aid. But beware. Don't fall into the trap of using jargon and in-house euphemisms (e.g., "persons of whom it is said they have different abilities"). You don't want your main points to be lost through a failure to speak clearly. Plus, the media will rarely use a jargon-laden description.

Ask the people you work with how they would like to be described

Nothing beats going directly to the source. When in doubt, ask some-one from the group you are advocating for to review your news release; he or she will catch any words that may cause you embarrassment. Remember, though, that brevity counts. A long description will usually be axed by the media in favour of a short one, even when the longer one is considered more sensitive by members of the group.

Develop guidelines to govern the way you report about others

A code of conduct for reporting, or just some simple do's and don'ts, will help people in your organization avoid making embarrassing errors.

Audience research

The communication efforts of many non-profit groups are like the actions of the hunter who shot his gun in the air every now and then in the hope that a duck would fly into a bullet. That kind of strategy will not do. You need to understand where your "ducks" are, how high they fly and what patterns they use. For that kind of information, you need to do research. The problem is that most non-profit groups don't have resources to pay for the kind of research that will give them information about their audience, what messages they are receptive to and what formats they want to hear it in.

But audience research doesn't have to be complicated or expensive. It can be as simple as handing out a flyer at the beginning of an event and asking people to fill it out and drop it off before leaving. A raffle is another way to find out what people think. After filling out the questionnaire, people enter the completed form in a draw. You might ask questions about the kind of media they use, magazines they subscribe to, issues that interest them, what they would like more information about, how they heard about your organization, and whether they think it is doing a good job.

Another easy way to survey supporters is through your annual request for funds. In addition to asking donors to fill out a form to update their contact information (mail and e-mail addresses), ask a few questions about the organization, its direction, and the quality of its programs and services. This will give you a sense of how well you are doing and any changes you may need to make in the future.

If you want to do more extensive research, contact companies that do surveys; most have non-profit rates. You can make it even more affordable by commissioning polling with some like-minded groups (e.g., several international development groups could survey opinions about foreign aid). Each group could ask a few specific questions about its organization, in addition to the general queries.

The result of this kind of research can be developed into a communication plan: a list of all the channels you will use to reach out to your supporters and the public at large (e.g., the media, a quarterly newsletter, an annual report, public meetings, donor letters, e-mail updates, website), when you will reach out to them and what you will say. Many colleges and universities offer communication courses for you to learn more about creating a communications plan.

Gimmicks

A communications director I know once sent a news release to the media wrapped around a bottle of beer. It must have worked, because a reporter I know still remembers receiving it. Finding ways to have your news release stand out from the pack is a goal of media relations, but you want to be careful about how you do it. The bottle of beer worked in this case, but it just as easily could have backfired. Some reporters might have seen it as a crass attempt to buy coverage. Even worse, it could have been addressed to a recovering alcoholic or a Muslim who, for religious reasons, abstains from drinking alcohol. Or what if the reporter who received it had lost a loved one to a drunk driver? The gimmick could have caused annoyance, anger and lack of coverage – the opposite of what was hoped.

There is an axiom in advertising – when it comes to humour, 25 per cent of people never get the joke. Most of these will just go "Huh?" but others may be offended. For this reason, be very careful about using gimmicks or jokes when you communicate with the media. What seems uproariously funny to you and your colleagues in the lunchroom may turn out to be a complete bomb in the newsroom. It could turn your news release – rather than the issue or event you are trying to promote – into news. Put it this way: if you, or anyone else in your organiza-tion, has any hesitation about the humour in your news release or the gimmick you want to employ, don't use it.

The Internet

The World Wide Web is an important part of your media relations strategy. Like most other people, reporters do research on the Web; it is also the place you can refer reporters to for more information about your organization. For this reason, you want to make sure that you have an updated and easy-to-use website.

Here are a few tips for creating a useful website.

Keep it simple

Plenty of companies out there will charge you lots of money to create a website with great graphics and all the bells and whistles. You may want a website that is complex and flashy, but it is not necessary. People come to the Web for information. They want to know what you do, how you do it, whom you serve, and how they can participate. The quality of your information is much more important than how eye-popping your graphics are. What is more, great graphics will not help if you don't offer anything of substance to visitors. The key thing is ease of use – whether people can quickly find the information they want.

People don't come to your site to be entertained; they come for the content. Be content-rich and you will keep them coming back.

Keep it up to date

When you create a website, you create a monster. Websites need to be updated regularly – once a month, if not more often. There is nothing worse than coming to a site and finding the words "Last updated June, 2002." If the people who created it don't care enough to put new information on the site, why should you care to visit it?

Being stagnant is one of the worst sins you can commit on the Web. In other words, once you commit to having a website, there is no turning back. You can keep it fresh by regularly adding items such as newsletters, articles, reports, letters from the president, the archbishop's monthly message, etc., on the site on a regular basis to keep it fresh. Remove older items when they are no longer relevant.

Many non-profit organizations gratefully accept the services of a volunteer who creates the site and keeps it updated. When the volunteer is hard-working, dedicated and can be counted on, this works out well. Other times, the outcome is less positive. The volunteer moves away or doesn't have time anymore and there is nobody to take his or her place. The result: your website languishes, getting older and staler by the day.

Since websites are such a vital part of the communications tool kit today, it is well worth it to pay someone on your staff to get basic Web training, the kind that will let him or her update the site on a regular basis. Or find out if your Internet service provider will, for a fee, do the updating for you. They may have a non-profit rate. Build this cost into your budget.

Respond promptly to e-mail

When people send e-mails to your organization, they expect to hear back immediately, if not sooner. Will someone at your organization take on this task? When people send you e-mails asking about how to volunteer or give, don't wait a week to respond to them. By then they may have moved on to another organization that responded more quickly.

Not all e-mails will be relevant to your work, of course, but all should get a reply, even if it is just "Thank you for your message. I can't help you with your query. Good luck tracking down the information you need." It is a simple courtesy, and takes only a minute or two.

Every website should provide a way for people to contact you by e-mail. Be warned, though. Putting e-mail addresses on a website is an invitation to receive spam, or unsolicited messages. A good way to prevent getting a mailbox full of junk is to create an e-mail address that spam robots can't read (at least, not yet), such as myorganizationatmyorganization.org (where the @ is spelled as "at"). People need to be instructed to remove the word "at" and replace it with @ when they send you an e-mail. You can also "hide" the e-mail address by just having the person's name appear on the page as a link (clicking on the name opens a new page in the visitor's e-mail program). Another way is to set up a general mailbox (myorganization@myorganization.org) that is checked by a staff member each day. This person then forwards messages to relevant staff. This way only one mailbox gets all the junk!

Promote your site in multiple ways

Some people will find your site by doing a search for your organization, faith group or issue. Others will find it through other means: on a brochure, on your letterhead, or in the signature on your e-mails. Don't count on a search engine to bring visitors to your site. Use as many channels as possible to promote it.

Include a search mechanism

An important feature to include on your website is a search mechanism. You may know exactly how to find information on the site, but a visitor might be confused. A search mechanism allows visitors to search your site by keyword, and then find every page that features that keyword.

Include a way of recording hits

One of the things the Web provides is feedback. Imagine being able to find out exactly which articles in a magazine or newspaper people read, and which they ignore, every time someone reads an issue – as if every time someone looked at an article that information was registered at your office and a mark placed beside the title. Over time you would discover which articles resonated with people and which ones didn't interest them. That is the kind of information you can gather when you provide a way of recording hits on your site. It is a great audience research tool, prompting questions about why some portions of your site get a lot of traffic and others get little.

Conclusion

The goal of this book is to help you and your organization get the media coverage you deserve and desire. But the larger goal is to help you share good news. People who work for non-profit organizations or religious groups are in the good news business – we are trying to make our neighbourhoods, communities, countries and world a better place to live. But bad news travels faster and farther than good news; it's much easier for the media to pick up. The good things that happen in the world often fly under the media's radar – unless someone brings it to their attention. That person is you.

Rick Salutin, a columnist for *The Globe and Mail*, put it this way: "At bottom, it is ordinary people, without ambitious personal agendas, who almost always remain a source of inspiration about human possibility, and tend to be responsible for whatever victories over arrogant power are won."

Our job as communicators is to help the ordinary people we serve and work with to tell their stories of human possibility. It is my hope that this book will let you accomplish that important goal.

About the Author

John Longhurst has worked in communications and media relations for various non-profit groups since 1981. The director of communications and marketing for Canadian Mennonite University in Winnipeg, Manitoba, he is also a columnist for the *Winnipeg Free Press*, writing on the Faith and View from the West pages, and a workshop leader on media relations for non-profit organizations. In 1998 he helped organize Canada's first-ever national conference on faith and the media. He also helped found the Centre for Faith and the Media.